Lessons from My Inner Teacher

Intuitive Journaling as a Tool for Growth

Sharon A. Brunink, Ph.D.

BALBOA.
PRESS
A DIVISION OF HAY HOUSE

Balboa Press books may be ordered through booksellers or by contacting:

Balboa Press
A Division of Hay House
1663 Liberty Drive
Bloomington, IN 47403
www.balboapress.com
1-(877) 407-4847

Because of the dynamic nature of the Internet, any web addresses or links contained in this book may have changed since publication and may no longer be valid. The views expressed in this work are solely those of the author and do not necessarily reflect the views of the publisher, and the publisher hereby disclaims any responsibility for them.

The author of this book does not dispense medical advice or prescribe the use of any technique as a form of treatment for physical, emotional, or medical problems without the advice of a physician, either directly or indirectly. The intent of the author is only to offer information of a general nature to help you in your quest for emotional and spiritual well-being. In the event you use any of the information in this book for yourself, which is your constitutional right, the author and the publisher assume no responsibility for your actions.

Any people depicted in stock imagery provided by Thinkstock are models, and such images are being used for illustrative purposes only. Certain stock imagery © Thinkstock.

Print information available on the last page.

ISBN: 978-1-4525-8194-1 (sc)
ISBN: 978-1-4525-8195-8 (hc)
ISBN: 978-1-4525-8196-5 (e)

Library of Congress Control Number: 2013916309

Balboa Press rev. date: 06/17/2016

Table of Contents

Lessons is dedicated, with gratitude, to all
our teachers and helpers, visible and invisible,
on every plane of consciousness.

Acknowledgments

I am grateful to my friends and family for their encouragement in seeing *Lessons* through to completion. To my Reiki practitioner friends, especially Sri Spielman, Laurie Mediavilla, Natalyi Selivanova, and Brenda Martinez, thank you for the unexpected, encouraging messages over the years. I am indebted to my author friend, Laura Feldman, and my psychotherapist friend, Mariette Losasso, for their kindness in reading the manuscript at different stages, offering feedback and reviews. My sister, Sally Vanderzyl, not only offered support but also provided helpful comments after reading the manuscript—thanks, Sally. To my fellow "morning pages" cohort and friend, Ginger Schnickel, I enjoy our shared journaling experiences more than you know. Huge thanks to Tony Ricci, my husband, for his confidence and support in my completing this book, even when I took work along on our travels.

Authors Henry Reed, and Kevin Todeschi graciously agreed to contribute reviews for *Lessons.* Thank you for your generosity and willingness to add one more thing to your busy schedules.

My outstanding editor, Colleen O'Brien, was a perfect match. I loved the fact that she has used and benefited from personal journaling for much of her life. Her precision in applying her knowledge of all aspects of editing is impressive.

I appreciated her positive outlook, reliability, and sense of humor. The formatting ideas she offered helped improve the book's layout and readability. I liked the fact that she did not shy away from posing difficult questions that encouraged me to dig deeper to clarify abstract concepts and my own personal reactions to some of the lessons. Many thanks, Colleen.

I am grateful to Frank DeVane, fellow writer and friend, for giving me the benefit of his input about publishing, helping troubleshoot computer glitches, and putting me in touch with Colleen. Many thanks to my friend, Susan Seager, who shared a way to transfer *Lessons* from my outdated computer to a new one.

To the professional team at Balboa Press, thank you for your ready availability, prompt and helpful responses to questions, your positive encouragement, and consistent checking in to help when needed. I greatly admired your professionalism throughout the entire process.

My heart-felt thanks to all of you and to my teachers in the world of spirit. This was truly a working partnership between the physical and spiritual planes of consciousness. I am deeply grateful for the wise knowledge and guidance from each lesson and the opportunity to be a vehicle for sharing these lessons with others.

Advance Reviews For
Lessons from My Inner Teacher
And Intuitive Journaling

"*Lessons from My Inner Teacher* is not only worth the read, it is worth keeping by your bed so you can handily return to it to glean one more piece of practical wisdom in order to live a happier life.

Author Brunink starts as skeptic; because of this, she makes this helpful little book completely believable and a relief to those who doubt the paranormal, feel foolish believing in it, or are afraid of what their friends will think of them if they do believe.

This book is set up first with solid steps on how to proceed, then come the words of the inner teacher herself, and then come the insightful comments on everything the author hears from the spiritual guide. The reader comes to like the humorous guide and the curious author. The spiritual advice is practical, covering everything from crankiness to the environment, from what others think to one's own belief in self, and a most hopeful statement on the world as we know it.

This is a remarkably helpful little book. What the inner teacher has to say about her/its own world of the spirit is fascinating and believable. What the inner teacher has to say about our world and how to handle it is simple; not necessarily easy, because we are so human—slow to get it, whatever it is; recalcitrant in most things; full of fear; and apt to procrastinate or fall asleep at important junctures in our lives—but what she teaches to ease our way is definitely within our grasp.

Even after the third read, I continued to find this book helpful, with new information and insights surfacing each time. What this means is that Brunink's book is not just a good read, it's a tool, a keeper, a resource for a long time."

Colleen Clopton, Writer

"In this thoughtful book peppered with insight and instruction, we share Dr. Brunink's inner world as she navigates an important life transition: retirement from her psychology practice. After years of regular meditation and journaling, she communicates with a spiritual teacher and guide who offer practical advice, dream interpretation, therapeutic suggestions, and a good helping of humor. I found this book inspiring, both because of the rich connection to the spirit world, and Sharon's innate wisdom in accomplishing a major personal change."

Laura Feldman, D.O.
Author of Heading for a Change of Light

"Dr. Sharon Brunink's unique and surprisingly easy intuitive journaling method is for anyone who seeks personal and spiritual growth. Brunink provides guidance and encouragement by sharing her own intuitive process and the wise lessons received through communication with her Higher Self. She writes with rare honesty, openness, and compassion. I use this powerful tool in my personal quest to practice mindful awareness. It helps me to live more fully from my true essence, with hope and humanity in my work as a psychotherapist. Free of technical jargon, full of wisdom and inspiration, this book is a gem!"

Mariette Losasso, MSN, APRN, PMHCNS-BC

Psychotherapist

"When Sharon first told me how I could receive answers to questions when I did not have someone handy to turn to, I was doubtful that I could do it. It seemed almost too simple—a source of help always at one's fingertips. So I decided to try my hand at intuitive journaling. Even the first attempt yielded positive results. I saw the wisdom in the answers. The words seemed to just flow. Sometimes words would simply pop into my mind. When I reread the responses, they were generally phrased in a style far more elegant and diplomatic than what I knew was my normal style. I find this journaling process a great comfort, knowing I have access to a higher wisdom whenever necessary."

Sri Spielman, Reiki Master

"One of the most important and yet oft-overlooked concepts in the Edgar Cayce material is the fact that each and every one of us has a wealth of guidance, inspiration, and counsel available to us at any time. That counsel comes from our own Higher Self—that Divine spark within each of us that maintains an affinity with the Creator—and can come to us in our dreams, in our meditations, in our inspired reflections, and in our creative pursuits. In this book, Brunink provides a wealth of information on how to access that creative Higher Self through inspirational writing and intuitive journaling. It is a book that has practical applications, especially during those moments in life when challenges and questions we face seem to be far more real and important than the overall splendor of life itself. I am fond of saying that we are ultimately employees for the Divine, charged with bringing spirit into the earth; Brunink's work provides practical tools to access that wisdom to help you fulfill that person for what your soul would have you be about."

Kevin J. Todeschi,
Executive Director and CEO, Edgar Cayce's Association
for Research and Enlightenment and Atlantic University
Author of *Edgar Cayce on the Akashic Records* and
Divine Encounters

Foreword

As we move from the 20th century to that of the 21st, it is becoming increasingly easier to envision the unconscious mind as being like outer space—infinite—rather than like an internal receptacle for holding our memories. In today's world, we discuss the non-local mind that is accessible directly from within. For many, it is the various demonstrations of this boundary-breaking aspect of mind that is most important and impressive—Let's see who comes through! For the more experienced, no more demonstration is needed. Rather, the interest is in creating a relationship with this resource in the hopes of improving one's life, maybe improving life on the planet. As Edgar Cayce— someone who developed a very constructive relationship with this resource—would often repeat, "Don't just be good, be good for *something!*"

You are holding a book that is offered both as a demonstration and as an offering of help, providing something useful for the reader to explore from within. *Lessons from My Inner Teacher: Intuitive Journaling as a Tool for Growth* has a lot to offer and it reads true to me. It's a great example of inspirational writing. The author is willing to take the more practical perspective, claiming humbly that she has gained a great deal of help from the process. In other words, it is practical. It could have been a simple way for her to introduce her work: I've found something that helps me—forget the explanation—you try it and see if it helps you too. That's the scientific process, pure and simple, and it works in the realm of spirituality too.

I have practiced the process the author describes. I wrote the book, *Edgar Cayce on Channeling Your Higher Self,* using essentially the same process but without the prayer of protection. I've learned from personal experience with this process that the best results come from putting into practice any lessons learned. In walking the thought, as it were, we grow into its truth. That follow-through tremendously empowers the creative process as well as the scientific process of discovery.

I wish the author had included more examples of how she applied the insights she gained. It is clear to me that the writing itself contains valid insights important for all of us to attempt to integrate. The author's personal reflections are as important to read as her intuitive journaling because it is in the reflections that she discusses what she has attempted to do with her insights.

As the author of *The Intuitive Heart* and having conducted research on how a grateful heart can perceive information seemingly invisible to the normal eye, I chose to study her chapters on that theme as a way of sampling the quality of her work. Lesson 5, for example, contains for me this provocative passage:

> *That's why focusing on the heart center with feelings of loving gratitude is so powerful. It's a*

uniting force or at least gives you the opportunity to touch the oneness and expansiveness associated with feelings of altruistic love. It's a way to connect with your soul and the spirit of oneness in all things. As such, it is the way back to your connection with Source.

This is an interesting approach to explaining the connection between gratitude and a consciousness of oneness. Because folks will attempt to practice gratitude in order to experience the blessings the author describes, it is important that Sharon also included some comments on her attempts to apply this insight. In her personal reflection for that lesson, she writes:

I am trying to remember to practice the heart exercise and maintain heart focus throughout the day as much as possible. I can definitely see the difference. When I am acting without heart focus, my mind and energy are scattered; there is a quality of inner tension and pressure associated with the task at hand. When I notice the tension and shift into an open-hearted focus and breathe into and out of the heart's gratitude, the effect is relaxing and my focus is clearer, sharper.

With this, Sharon reports the insight seems to work when she remembers to apply it. She suggests that using her breath helps as a way to shift her frame of mind, thus expanding upon what she received in her writing.

To me, that interaction between her inspirations and her perspirations give the book a more grounded authenticity. I approve! I think Sharon's writing stands on its own. It reads valid to me as coming from her—our?—Higher Self. Nevertheless, don't get entranced by where it comes from. Better to sit in prayer and then write a letter to yourself from your Higher Self—and follow its' advice!

My suggestion for the reader, therefore, is to read, enjoy, and ponder the many insights that are in this worthwhile and constructive book. Choose a few and attempt to follow them in your life. Most importantly, begin the process of spontaneous writing as the author describes in this important book, and look forward to your own insights and how you can grow into them, day by day.

Henry Reed, Ph.D., Director,
The Edgar Cayce Institute for Intuitive Studies
Author of *Channeling Your Higher Self*
and *The Intuitive Heart*

Introduction

What if you discovered you had ready access to a rich, unlimited source of knowledge and wisdom to guide your learning and growth? What if you also found that this source of wisdom and knowledge was already within you, waiting to be discovered and used at your request?

Lessons from My Inner Teacher resulted from my consciously tapping into this inner source of wisdom, the higher Self, through use of intuitive journaling. After hearing what my inner teacher had to say, I decided to share these lessons I received from the world of spirit and to teach others how to use intuitive journaling to connect with their own inner guidance and wisdom.

Intuitive journaling is a conscious, intentional way of communicating with our higher Self, the soul, and a higher source of wisdom. Since our higher Self and the world of spirit are part of the field of universal consciousness unlimited by time or space, we all have access to its knowledge, wisdom, and guidance. I came to think of this knowledge and wisdom accessed from a higher source through my higher Self as my inner teacher.

Journaling and writing have long been tools for reflection and inner exploration in the human quest to know and understand who we are and the meaning and purpose of our lives.

My personal use of journaling began in 2002 with "morning pages," a form of writing developed by Julia Cameron in *The Artist's Way* and Bryan, Cameron and Allen's *The Artist's Way at Work.*

Morning pages, as described by Cameron in *The Artist's Way,* are simply three handwritten pages each morning of uninterrupted writing of whatever comes to mind. As suggested would happen, this daily practice of morning pages and the self-exploration exercises led me to a more conscious connection with my higher Self and its rich source of inner wisdom. The attuning with my higher Self to communicate with a higher source of wisdom contained within that infinite field of universal consciousness led me to my inner teacher. This source of wisdom and knowledge is unlimited in scope. It is always available within to foster our growth as spiritual beings and fulfillment of our life purposes.

Connection with my inner teacher evolved from consistent use of this form of journaling. It was as helpful when used in an open-ended way for whatever was most needed at that time as when used in a focused way to resolve difficult situations, relationships, or negative emotions. Through my inner teacher, I was able to access deeper levels of knowledge and wisdom. The astute guidance I received helped me see more clearly my life path, its challenges, and how to deal with them in positive ways.

There are, of course, other tools for accessing inner wisdom for self-healing and growth. One such tool I made use of in my clinical practice and in my personal life was guided imagery as taught by Martin Rossman. This technique uses a guided, structured script to assist with creating a relaxed state that allows you to access a wise inner advisor for help in understanding symptoms, a specific problem, or new ways to view and change difficult situations. This is done through paying attention to inner images that may come in thoughts, words, pictures, sensations, and feelings while in a relaxed state and focusing on the concern you wish to understand. After the guided imagery exercise is completed, a written record of the experience is made to assess progress over time. Readers interested in this approach may wish to consult Rossman's excellent self-help book, *Guided Imagery for Self-Healing*.

Like guided imagery, intuitive journaling is done from a relaxed, centered state and involves recording the inner thoughts, words, pictures, sensations, feelings, and direct knowings that arise. I found that journaling by itself was the most efficient and powerful way of accessing this wise inner teacher for help with specific problems. With intuitive journaling, the preparation is self-directed; recording occurs as the inner experience unfolds. This powerful method of working with recurring issues proved so useful I eventually made it part of my daily journaling. I normally started daily journaling with a shortened version of Cameron's morning pages and then transitioned into intuitive journaling with the process described below.

Cameron stated that it is not possible to write morning pages for an extended time without connecting with this inner source of wisdom or the Creator within. Because of this, she viewed morning pages as a spiritual practice. *Lessons* presents the powerful spiritual lessons I received from my own connection and communication with this inner source of wisdom through intuitive journaling. From my perspective, intuition is synonymous with the higher Self or soul, and I use these terms interchangeably. Intuitive journaling, then, could also be seen as the soul's wisdom expressed in written form.

While working on preparing this manuscript for publication, I came across an article on inspirational writing by Joanne DiMaggio in the 2011 issue of *Venture Inward*, the magazine of Edgar Cayce's Association for Research and Enlightenment. Soon after, I read Henry Reed's book, *Channeling Your Higher Self,* also based on Cayce's readings, which included a section on inspirational writing. Despite my familiarity with Edgar Cayce's philosophy and readings, I was unaware of his concept of inspired writing until then. I was struck by the similarities between inspirational writing as a transpersonal writing tool and what I call intuitive journaling. DiMaggio describes inspirational writing as a method of communicating with a Higher Source through the soul's guidance which inspires us to look within for answers. This is how I view intuitive journaling.

I do not claim any scientific proof or objective data observable with our five physical senses to support my conclusions regarding the source of this intuitive information. My direct experience through the use of inner, nonphysical senses—often called extrasensory perception—brought about an inner knowing neither directly observable nor provable in a strictly scientific sense that I was in touch with something that was universal, limitless, and profound. Needless to say, I have found using this intuitive inner wisdom immeasurably helpful in my own life and growth.

In the end, direct experience of the knowledge, inspiration, and quality of lessons contained in the material and the results of their application in daily life were of greater importance than being able to provide objective, scientific proof. However, I was still curious about whether this internal experience in which I was able to tap a higher wisdom could be understood in the context of more current quantum physics concepts. With that in mind, I included an appendix that cites references helpful in my understanding of this inner experience from a scientific perspective.

This book is based on a series of intuitive lessons I received and transcribed from October 19, 2006 through January 25, 2007. This time frame coincided with the last few months of my professional practice as a clinical psychologist as I prepared for retirement. These lessons resulted from a consistent intention on my part to connect and communicate with my higher Self and a higher wisdom within so I could learn and grow, personally and spiritually.

It is my belief that we all have access to this source of wisdom within through our higher Self. Some of us are more aware of this inner resource than others. All of us, with regular practice, can learn to consciously develop reliable ways to tap in to and use this vast inner storehouse of knowledge and wisdom whenever we choose.

Aside from basic editing, changes in personal information to protect privacy, simplifying sentence structure, and elimination of the repetitive beginning phrase, the lessons that follow are exact transcriptions. I transcribed each lesson using my own personal shorthand at the time I intuitively received the information. I was fully awake as I recorded the experiences as they flowed through my inner senses.

I established a series of steps to prepare for intuitive journaling to make the process consistent and easier to remember. To remind the reader of the process used to establish communication with my inner teacher in preparation for intuitive journaling, I have repeated these steps before each of the first five lessons. After the preparatory steps, all chapters begin with the actual edited, dated transcript for that day's lesson. Each lesson is titled to reflect its dominant theme. Most lessons are followed with my personal reflections regarding that day's lessons and intuitive experience as well as updated information added during the editing process.

The bracketed italics within the lessons represent my personal comments, added during the editing process for publication. Their purpose is to clarify for the reader my internal reactions when it seemed relevant to understanding the lesson.

My preparation for and completion of each day's intuitive journaling was the same over the course of these lessons. What follows is a step-by-step description of what I typically did and its purpose.

- First, I started with twenty to thirty minutes of meditation or, when this was not possible, a brief centering exercise with deep breathing to relax and focus inward. This helped calm and quiet the body-mind, allowing it to slide into neutral and let go of the ego self and its concerns. The resulting shift into a nonthinking, expansive meditative state helped facilitate connection with the higher Self and the highest source of wisdom to which it led me.

- Second, I dated each journaling session and began with a shorter version of typical morning pages, as I had done for several years with Cameron's *The Artist's Way,* simply writing stream of consciousness thoughts as they appeared in my mind. This was calming and centering as it helped dump any remaining concerns about the day ahead. The morning pages journaling are not part of *Lessons.*

- Third, when the five to ten minutes of morning pages seemed complete, I shifted into intuitive journaling. I began every intuitive journaling session with this written intention and request: intention set for pure, clear, accurate connection and communication with highest wisdom regarding whatever is most needed at this time. Later on, as I became more familiar with this open-ended intention process, I added specific concerns or questions for which I was requesting help. Writing these out each time served the purpose of clearly communicating my request as well as my intention to be open to listening to and receiving information from the highest source of wisdom without preconceived ideas or expectations. It also provided a written record of each session and any input on specific issues for which I was seeking help.

At the beginning, I used the open-ended format of asking for what was most needed at that time to avoid limiting information, and to tap into my higher Self's guidance about what was needed right then. Later, I was more at ease adding specific requests for help with difficult situations, understanding dreams or other intuitive experiences, and clarifying the meaning of certain life experiences.

- Fourth, the written intention was followed by a brief prayer of protection. I silently repeated the following prayer which I adapted from Edgar Cayce's prayer of protection suggested for meditation: As I open my heart, mind, and spirit to the unseen Divine forces around the throne of grace, mercy, and might, I am surrounded by the pure light of protection found in the thought of the Christ Consciousness. The term Christ Consciousness is not meant in a religious sense. It refers to the universal pattern of consciousness that applies to all humanity, regardless of one's religious beliefs.

I encourage readers to form intentions and prayers of protection that are meaningful to them and grounded in high spiritual ideals. Examples of ideals aligned with the higher Self as opposed to the ego self include unconditional love versus ego-conditional love and judgment; highest wisdom or highest good of all versus me-mine; use for genuine growth, learning, and service versus use for entertainment, impressing others, or setting oneself apart as better than others. I offer what I did only as an example. In establishing a connection and communication with the highest source of inner wisdom, grounding your request and intention in your highest spiritual ideals is important, from my perspective, because like attracts like. What you focus on and intend directs your energy, drawing to you what is similar. This is a way of being consciously aware of and integrating the ideals that you wish to inform and guide your life and personal development.

These preparatory steps following meditation or centering and morning pages take approximately one and a half minutes once you become familiar with them. The process is actually much simpler than it appears from the number of pages needed to give a clear, step-by-step description so you can do this on your own.

- Fifth, I had two ways I typically began the fifteen to twenty minutes of intuitive writing after the intention and prayer of protection. Sometimes I wrote down the starter phrase, If my higher Self/ soul spoke to me now, then immediately recorded whatever thoughts I heard from my inner teacher with no attempt to direct what I received. When the inner flow of communication lessened or stopped, it felt done. Many times, my inner teacher would indicate this by saying in thoughts, "That's enough for today."

More often, after the prayer of protection, I simply listened within and sensed the connection with my inner teacher. The connection was confirmed when I mentally heard her beginning phrase, "I am here with you." I came to recognize this beginning phrase, accompanied by her brief, positive comment such as, "Thank you for showing up," as a signal that my connection with my higher Self and inner teacher was established and the intuitive communication process had begun.

As I mentally sensed the beginning phrase in my mind, I could simultaneously feel my inner teacher's presence. Personal qualities such as warmth, kindness, clarity, gentleness, strength, and humor were evident. These attributes, perceived with the nonphysical senses, seemed clearer and stronger than those experienced in physical life interactions. I then simply recorded the information as it was conveyed through my inner senses until it came to an end and we said goodbye.

My inner teacher communicated by way of direct thought so that I had the feeling of inner knowing. She responded to my unspoken mental questions or even vague wonderings as soon as I thought them. There is no way to describe how awesome in the true definition of the word this unspoken, interactive experience of mind-to-mind communication was while at the same time feeling quite natural.

The intuitive journaling usually continued for about twenty minutes unless my schedule necessitated a shorter time.

- Sixth, at the end of my intuitive journaling, when my schedule allowed, I recorded personal observations and relevant events. These form the basis for the personal reflection section that follows most of the intuitive lessons as well as some of the bracketed comments within the lessons. During the editing process, I also added more current information and observations to update the material in the personal reflections section.

Intuitive journaling is not automatic writing. My understanding of automatic writing is that the impressed or channeled material comes from outside the self while the writer is in a trance. Intuitive writing comes from within for the intended purpose of furthering spiritual growth and is not written from a trance state. It is a way of tapping into inner wisdom from an infinite source within that is accessible to all of us through our higher Self or soul. People have a variety of beliefs about the origin of this wisdom: God; angels, Masters, or other enlightened beings; spirit guides; higher Self or the soul; the subconscious or superconscious mind; Divine or Infinite Mind; All That Is; the Akashic records; or akashic consciousness. In my view, these are simply different ways of describing our connection with universal consciousness, the divine light of unconditional love that permeates and animates all of life.

I discovered that an attitude of open receptivity—allowing the intuitive writing process to flow—worked best. This attitude defines what I think is meant by getting the ego out the way or letting go of the left brain tendency to analyze. Typically, I am a logical thinker who approaches tasks in an organized, linear way so that I can complete things efficiently. So, learning to shift out of my analytical thinking style to one of going with the flow required practice as well as suspension of disbelief. My meditation practice and regular use of guided relaxation, imagery, and visualization techniques were helpful in bringing a detached, allowing, observing attitude into this intuitive writing.

I rarely reread the daily lesson entries until much later. Whenever I did look at them I always learned something new. I developed this habit from Cameron advising writers of morning pages to set them aside without reviewing them until perhaps several months later. Intuitively, this fit my own response to completing a journaled lesson. Once it was done I had no desire to read it until much later. Since I used my own personal shorthand to record verbatim the mind-to-mind communication occurring in the intuitive lessons, I knew an accurate written record was available anytime I needed it. I was consistently surprised at the content and quality of the material when I reread it. It fit perfectly with the circumstances at the time I recorded it and provided a depth of knowledge that would never have occurred to me. The clear, compassionate way the lessons were expressed far surpassed anything I had ever written. It was distinctly different from my own voice.

Never in my wildest imagining did I envision authoring such a book. I have come to see the recurring doubts and fears that emerged throughout the lessons as a natural part of the resistance and acceptance process that occurs with any major change involving a shift in awareness and the growth that flows naturally from such changes. I expected and would have preferred these intuitive lessons to remain private. I was unprepared for the statement from my inner teacher that these lessons were meant to be made public for the benefit of others. Quite frankly, I dismissed it at the time. But, here it is. I could not in good conscience decline to make this available to others who could benefit as I have.

As I found this way of learning and growing delightful and uplifting to experience, it also gives me a measure of delight to share it with others in the hope they are equally, if not more, delighted.

If you have chosen to read this book, it is also my hope you will learn something new and be inspired to develop, strengthen, and use the connection with your own inner source of wisdom to guide your growth and learning.

LESSON ONE

Making Contact

Preparatory Steps for Intuitive Journaling

Meditate or center

Enter date and time in journal

Write out intention in journal: intention set for pure, clear, accurate connection and communication with highest wisdom regarding whatever is most needed at this time followed by any specific concerns or questions for which you are requesting help

Repeat prayer of protection: As I open my heart, mind, and spirit to the unseen Divine forces around the throne of grace, mercy, and might, I am surrounded by the pure light of protection found in the thought of the Christ Consciousness.

Begin writing using starter phrase: If my soul or higher Self spoke to me now, and continue writing whatever comes to mind until it stops.

10/19/06, 7:30 a.m., Lesson One

I am here. I have much to tell you. Thank you for opening your heart and mind to me. It's easiest if I speak in thoughts. You'll find a way that works best for you to record this for your and others' benefit.

Don't try so hard. It works more easily if you allow your mind and heart to open and receive. *[As soon as she spoke this, I noticed how much inner tension and tightness I was creating with my attitude that I had to control this process. This simple awareness helped me shift into a relaxed openness in my heart center.]*

It's okay to question and is preferred. *[Good to know. I have lots of questions.]*

You're curious about who I am. *[That's an understatement!]* That will wait for another, later time. *[Okay. I trust there's a reason for that.]*

I don't want to tire you so I will let you set the pace for this work. All that's needed is for you to sit quietly, say your prayer of protection, and ask me to be present. Then we'll begin work. I'm pleased to have this chance to teach you and others what I know.

You'll know you are truly connected with an enlightened source of wisdom from the gentle, compassionate manner in which I appear; the fact that I will never force on you something you did not request or are unwilling to cooperate with; and I will never do or say anything belittling or critical or harm you in any way. *[My inner teacher's manner and tone in communicating totally embodied these qualities despite my skeptical thoughts beginning this endeavor. This greatly relieved me about how I'd tell if I was connected with an enlightened source. That is the reason for the prayer of protection, but I clearly didn't trust it or myself completely.]*

You will sense the truth of this as you do now. If you surround yourself with protection and in your prayer ask or invite only the highest wisdom from the Christ Consciousness, you will be safe, and other less enlightened souls will not be able to influence or harm you. *[I took the reference to less enlightened souls to mean disembodied souls that remain earthbound or less enlightened souls on the lower astral planes which Cayce and other metaphysical writers describe. I intuitively understood the reference to harm not in the physical sense but as harm caused by being led astray from my intended purpose of connecting with highest wisdom.]*

You can insure that this work stays accurate and pure by simply opening, listening, and recording what you hear mentally in thoughts during our designated work time; by continuing meditation to foster your own spiritual development; and by avoiding interpreting what is said. *[The process of writing everything I hear with my nonphysical, inner hearing takes all my mental attention so my analyzing, interpreting mind is in neutral mode. I just write what I receive.]*

This is a true working partnership. I'm honored to have this vehicle to teach you and others.

Yes, I sense and hear your thoughts and mental questions, and I respond with thoughts you hear with your inner mind. *[This was my inner teacher's immediate response to my wondering if she knows my thoughts as I think them.*

Oddly enough, I find this delightful, even comforting, as there has been no judgment or criticism regarding some of the outrageous thoughts I've already had like "my family and colleagues will disown me; they'll think I've lost my mind or am making this up. What if I am?" No matter how fearful my thoughts, all were met only with acceptance. Also, I appreciated the bottom line integrity and directness of not having to peel through facades, pretenses, and defenses. You get what's there, right away. Don't get me wrong. This coming up against one's inner negative thoughts is not easy or pleasant, but it certainly allows lots of opportunities for honest self-examination.]

Your eagerness to know everything right away mirrors my own eagerness to teach. But as you sense and see in your inner mind, I am more patient with this process than you're able to be right now. I know that it's best to allow things to emerge at the right time. So when I hold back or delay informing you of something you want to know, it's because the timing is not yet right. *[I have to laugh at how kindly she refers to my impatience and my attitude of wanting to know everything immediately even though I know that would be ridiculously overwhelming. Her patience for right timing is a great model for me.]*

This is enough for today and spells out the process for our working together when you are able. *[I found this plenty to take in, as it is challenging to remain open in this way while also making a written record. Plus, most days I had limited time before work or other commitments. So the time allotted for this seemed just right. Though I had a sense of positive satisfaction after completing today's lesson, I had no thought of sharing it with others just yet and was surprisingly emotionally neutral about it.]*

Have a wonderful day. You can do so by thinking and affirming this with assured intention. *[I intuitively sensed that my teacher was reminding me of the power of our thoughts and intentions. I liked that she encouraged me to use this in approaching my day. I still do this; it sets a positive, relaxed tone for the day. One example of such an affirmed intention is: I choose to bring to all my days' events, activities, and interactions an attitude of wonder, joy, and gratitude.]*

Personal Reflections

This first lesson gave me clues about what it would be like working together with my inner teacher in this intuitive journaling. Most often, I used an open-ended format of simply listening within and writing what I heard. Our communication always began with her thought, "I am here" or "I am here with you." I sensed and heard her voiced thoughts like an internal conversation with my nonphysical, inner senses. Though no words were ever spoken aloud, her voice, which I experienced as inner thoughts, was distinctly different from my own. I came to recognize this beginning phrase as confirmation of my connection with my higher Self or soul, my inner teacher, and a higher source of wisdom.

I have retained this beginning phrase, "I am here," for the first five lessons as a reminder for the reader but, except for a couple of occasions, eliminated it after that.

My inner teacher's voice and personal qualities were even more distinctive and clearly experienced with my inner, nonphysical senses than if she were physically present. She had a strong, confident, peaceful, unrushed presence and a gentle voice. I had a palpable sense of her expansive warmth, caring, strength, and patience. Though sure of herself and her knowledge, she conveyed it in a humble manner. She was clear in her communication of information; authoritative without being authoritarian; respectful; and considerate.

My inner teacher made it clear I would set the pace for this joint working partnership based on my time and energy level. She also clarified the simple process needed to begin the communication and insure its accuracy. Although she acknowledged my curiosity and mental questions about her, she elected not to answer these queries until the timing was right for such information to emerge. Surprisingly, I accepted this explanation without question as I understood the concept of timely delivery of information. I intuitively understood that such questions about who and what she was, though valid, would be a major distraction from the lessons to be communicated. As I was already skeptical enough about the validity of the communication received, waiting until I was further along in accepting this form of intuitive guidance made sense. I laughed, though, at the lesson in patience, since patience is not my strongest suit. It motivated me to practice patience mindfully every day.

I realized my inner teacher knew exactly what my current state of mind was as well as my unspoken questions and wonderings as she addressed these instantly and directly as they occurred. Examples of this included her knowing and responding to my inner feelings even when I was out of touch with them; responding to my unspoken questions regarding who she was and how to insure the information being received was true and accurate; and coaching me about the best way to approach this intuitive communication process.

I recorded verbatim what I heard in my mind and thoughts from my inner teacher. I realized much later that the recording process so occupied my attention that it served as a distraction for my analytical mind, allowing me to stay in a neutral state of receiving.

The experience of receiving a voice through unspoken thoughts and having my thoughts and mental questions instantaneously heard and responded to without ever speaking aloud was delightful and freeing. Sentences beginning with yes in the transcriptions denote such experiences of immediate responses to mental wonderings I was aware of having at that time. Communicating with the inner senses did not appear to be limited by time or space. The experience of hearing, seeing, and feeling with the inner senses was immediate. The usual facades we present in the external world did not exist here. Subterfuge and dishonesty were not possible as true inner thoughts and feelings were immediately evident as they occurred.

LESSON TWO

How Intuitive Journaling Works

Preparatory Steps for Intuitive Journaling

<u>Meditate or center</u>

<u>Enter date and time in journal</u>

<u>Write out intention in journal</u>: intention set for pure, clear, accurate connection and communication with highest wisdom regarding whatever is most needed at this time followed by any specific concerns or questions for which you are requesting help

<u>Repeat prayer of protection</u>: As I open my heart, mind, and spirit to the unseen Divine forces around the throne of grace, mercy, and might, I am surrounded by the pure light of protection found in the thought of the Christ Consciousness.

<u>Begin writing using starter phrase</u>: If my soul or higher Self spoke to me now, and continue writing whatever comes to mind until it stops.

10/20/06, 7:30 a.m., Lesson Two

I am here. Thank you for showing up. I know you have limited time today so we'll be brief. *[This is an example of my inner teacher knowing and using personal details about me in a considerate way. I wonder who "we" is; I trust I'll find that out when the time is right.]*

Trust what comes. Our work together is intended to be published and it is being given with that in mind. *[This is a surprise. Not exactly what I had in mind. Still, it's early on so I'll wait and see where this takes me. I already know it's my choice and that my inner teacher will not judge my eventual decision or tell me what to do, as she made this clear in lesson one. Seems like my inner teacher may have a bigger purpose in giving these lessons of which I was unaware.]*

We'll help with that process. *[Again, I wonder who this "we" is but understand intuitively that she is referring to help with the publication process. Since it's early on, I'm able to set it aside for now. Just in case this is true and I'm not making this up, I silently say thanks for the offered help, as I'll need all the help I can get if I decide to publish something so private.]*

Your part will be to keep a good record as you are now doing. *[That's manageable. I can do that.]*

Though you cannot see me in that I am not visible to your outer senses, I am still present there with you just as surely as if I were there with you physically. It's the same. For you to remain open to receiving my teaching, stay tuned in to my presence just as you would give a friend in physical form

9

your undivided attention when they're with you. *[Yes, my attention sometimes drifts during my inner communication with my teacher as it does with real life communication with family and friends. But I notice I can pause the inner communication with my teacher when I need, for example, to take a bathroom break. I simply restart the information flow by silently indicating my readiness to continue. Due to the novelty of the way intuitive communication occurs, the content that comes through, and having to write quickly to get everything down accurately, sustaining attention is not as difficult as I expected. If I'm distracted by personal concerns or a negative mood, these are addressed by my inner teacher in the form of a lesson. On the occasions I am distracted, I use the meditation strategy of returning attention to my focus on my inner teacher as soon as I notice my attention has wandered. My inner teacher forces nothing. She waits for me to return my attention when this is necessary.]*

Since you sense, feel, and see me with only your inner senses, it's easy to let your attention drift. If it helps, picture me there with you in your mind's eye much as your successful patients learn to internalize the therapy process and connect with their inner helper/wisdom with use of visualization. The process is similar—can you see that? *[This refers to an event from yesterday which I mention in the personal reflection notes below where a patient described using an internalized visualization of her therapy session to eliminate a panic attack. It's an inventive metaphor as the inner process is indeed quite similar. I would not have put that together on my own.]*

Except yours *[yesterday's event]* occurs in the physical dimension and this *[intuitive communication]* is coming to you from the spiritual dimension.

Most people are unaware that such communication is possible because they either do not acknowledge a spiritual dimension, see it as inaccessible to them while living on earth, or don't trust their ability to be in touch with and communicate with the spiritual dimension. All people do that in dreams without their being aware of it. We're going to use it deliberately, and, as with everything else, your skill at this will improve and develop with practice. *[This is truly an awesome way of being stretched out of your comfort zone!]*

Think of this communication between us as your inner experience of the spiritual dimension using visualization and imagination in the form of mental imagery to connect with and learn from those of us who are teachers in the spiritual dimension. *[This suggests my inner teacher is a being from spirit, communicating and teaching through my higher Self.]*

Personal Reflections

My work schedule was tight today and, as a result, I was a bit more scattered and tense. Despite this, I still felt a clear sense of my inner teacher's warmth, kindness, and clarity during today's intuitive communication. By comparison, however, I noticed that yesterday's intuitive experience of these personal qualities of my inner teacher was stronger as I was more relaxed and focused. This makes sense from the perspective that the strength and clarity of internal intuitive experiences are affected by one's level of relaxation or tension.

Yesterday, I saw a past patient who described using the following process to successfully manage severe panic attacks on her own: sitting in a chair she has designated her therapy chair, she used deep breathing to relax then visualized a therapy session in which she discussed what she needed to face and how to constructively cope with events triggering her extreme anxiety. Her use of positive visualization of past therapy sessions allowed her to access her own inner wisdom regarding what was needed to understand and eliminate her feelings of panic. My teacher's metaphoric use of this event to describe and clarify what was occurring in our intuitive communication and working partnership was ingenious. This made me realize my inner teacher seemed to know everything about me even when we were not in direct contact or I was not consciously aware of certain thoughts and feelings. I also realized that my inner teacher used my professional experiences as a clinical psychologist to frame today's lesson. In fact, this construction of lessons around my personal and professional interests and relationships was evident throughout. Though the lessons seem to me to be universal in nature, the ways they are presented are unique to each writer. The lessons I received are clearly tailored to me and what I need to learn.

The intimate knowledge my inner teacher seemed to have of me and use in the lessons left me wondering how this is possible. How does this inner experience of the spiritual dimension using intention, intuition, and alignment with the higher Self help me connect with teachers in the spiritual dimension? Is this part of what is meant by the oneness of all life or the universal consciousness? Why does meditation help facilitate such intuitive, extrasensory communication? Is there something about the meditative state of mind that helps develop an energetic resonance with higher states of consciousness, the higher Self, or the spiritual dimension? If the higher Self or soul is that eternal part of each of us that has access to all knowledge and wisdom because it is part of the All, the Infinite Mind, then such communication between me in the physical world and invisible teachers from the spiritual world would seem possible.

LESSON
THREE

Spirit Is Universal Love

Preparatory Steps for Intuitive Journaling

<u>Meditate or center</u>

<u>Enter date and time in journal</u>

<u>Write out intention in journal</u>: intention set for pure, clear, accurate connection and communication with highest wisdom regarding whatever is most needed at this time followed by any specific concerns or questions for which you are requesting help

<u>Repeat prayer of protection</u>: As I open my heart, mind, and spirit to the unseen Divine forces around the throne of grace, mercy, and might, I am surrounded by the pure light of protection found in the thought of the Christ Consciousness.

<u>Begin writing using starter phrase</u>: If my soul or higher Self spoke to me now, and continue writing whatever comes to mind until it stops.

10/22/06, 8 p.m., Lesson Three

I am here. You are anxious, needlessly. You fear this is not real and there will be nothing to say. Let this go. Trust the process, believe. Effort is not necessary. All that is needed is relaxed openness, receptivity of your heart and mind. The teachings come through me to you as the vessel.

Doubt and disbelief block my voice and you are unable to hear me. To open your heart and mind, focus on your heart center and the feeling of love and gratitude. Imagine the love and gratitude flowing upward from your heart to the mind (i.e., center of the brain, pineal gland), then downward from the mind to the heart like a circling wheel.

God is love; the universe is love. You cut yourselves off from this universal love much in the same way your doubts, disbelief, intensity, and effort block your ability to hear or sense me with your inner senses. Awareness of universal love—God Consciousness—requires receptivity and a relaxed openness of heart and mind. Yes, in response to your mental question, that's why the stillness and quieting of the mind and thoughts in meditation are important. It's the path to an open heart and mind. It allows for a deep connection with the universal consciousness as well as these teachings from the dimension of spirit. These dimensions are always present. People's doubts, fears, ignorance, and closed hearts and minds all block awareness of and communication with spirit. So do lack of faith and belief. Nothing harmful will come from your connection with the spirit dimension. You are protected and only the highest sources of wisdom can be received. *[This relates to two concepts mentioned earlier: first, the importance of grounding my intention in a high spiritual ideal as like attracts like, and what I focus on directs my energy and draws to me that which is similar; and, second, the observations and cautions in metaphysical and spiritual writing regarding the potential for accessing less enlightened sources of information which are not loving or wise—disembodied souls who remain earthbound or less developed souls on the lower astral plane.]*

The world of spirit is the world of universal love. It stimulates the desire to learn, create, help, and serve others. Those are all manifestations of love. There is no competition with this. Learning and skills are shared with those who ask and are not withheld. This is an expression of universal love. The gentleness, compassion, and care you sense in me are manifestations of universal love or God. It is present everywhere and in every thing. Your inability to see or connect with it is because you have forgotten your Source and lost your awareness that you are one with universal love or God Consciousness. That is the natural state of your spirit, and your soul is ever guiding you back to that awareness. *[It is my belief that we are all one with this universal consciousness, whether or not we are aware of it. It is our disconnection from the infinite light of love within that creates forgetting and separation. I believe that the task of all humanity is to reconnect with and live physical life from this Source of universal love within, the soul, for the purpose of reflecting back the unique expression of our soul's light and love to the interconnected oneness of All That Is.]*

That's enough for tonight. Perhaps morning when you're fresher would be a better time for us to do this work.

Personal Reflections

This third intuitive lesson was done after Sunday evening's meditation. I was tired after a stimulating weekend with a friend visiting from out of town. Despite increased tension resulting from my fatigue and doubts about whether the information received during intuitive journaling is real, I still sensed the strong presence of warmth and peacefulness from my inner teacher during today's lesson. A wealth of information flowed through. I plan to make every effort to do this in the mornings when I'm fresher and evaluate how that works compared to later in the day, the only alternate time I have available. My visitor, trained both conventionally and in Chinese medicine, pointed out during our weekend together that nighttime is for closing metabolically and energetically, whereas daytime is for opening. This gives subjective validity to the terms winding down and gearing up that we use to describe our days. It also provides another explanation of why this connection and communication flows more easily early in the day.

Quieting the mind and thoughts through meditation is one way of creating the relaxed openness of heart-mind that allows for connection with the higher Self or soul. One of the best, brief descriptions of a variety of meditation practices is Joan Borysenko's beautiful book, *Pocketful of Miracles.* Readers interested in exploring different spiritual practices to find a good personal fit for quieting the mind and connecting with inner stillness may find Borysenko's appendix of meditation practices helpful. Other excellent writers on meditation include Pema Chodron and Jon Kabat-Zinn.

**LESSON
FOUR**

*The Power of Living
from a Grateful Heart*

Preparatory Steps for Intuitive Journaling

<u>Meditate or center</u>

<u>Enter date and time in journal</u>

<u>Write out intention in journal</u>: intention set for pure, clear, accurate connection and communication with highest wisdom regarding whatever is most needed at this time followed by any specific concerns or questions for which you are requesting help

<u>Repeat prayer of protection</u>: As I open my heart, mind, and spirit to the unseen Divine forces around the throne of grace, mercy, and might, I am surrounded by the pure light of protection found in the thought of the Christ Consciousness.

<u>Begin writing using starter phrase</u>: If my soul or higher Self spoke to me now, and continue writing whatever comes to mind until it stops.

10/23/06, 3:30 p.m., Lesson Four

I am here. It's so hard for you to trust this process. *[This refers, once again, to my inflexible insistence on an orderly preparation.]* You are used to a perfectionist way of doing things which is helpful in assuring quality, best effort, and conscientiousness in tending to our work. For example, you have shown up to work even when you're having doubts about whether this is real. Thank you for that. There's a lot to be said for showing up no matter what and doing your best. Yet a simple prayer and visualized protection is all that's needed followed by letting me know you're ready to work. I am always here and available, ready for this work whenever you are.

I know you want me to identify a topic and keep this process structured. Stay open to doing this in ways other than that. I know it's uncomfortable not to have the structure of topics with a linear progression in our teachings or a chance to prepare as you typically do. So this will be lots of practice in simply staying open to what is at the moment. You would call it going with the flow. We refer to it as being and living in the present and trusting that process completely. There is no time here in the dimension of spirit, so we are not bound by deadlines or time pressure.

I know you want to name me and know everything about me. Be patient and try to let go of controlling this process. Yes, focusing on your heart center helps with letting go of over-thinking, analyzing, planning, and directing. It also helps with staying present to this moment. *[The sentence beginning with "yes" was another example of my teacher's answering my unspoken question about whether heart-focused breathing would help move me out of my thinking mind.]*

It's easier for me to communicate with you when you're focused on your heart center or are in a state of love. That necessarily makes us present only to that experience. Being in a state of love can be developed and enhanced with heart focus. As you know from the Institute of HeartMath's research, the heart's electromagnetic rhythm is what sets the rhythm for all body systems including the brain. The heart determines whether the body-mind is working together in a balanced, synergistic way. The heart center is very powerful; thoughts of love and gratitude can enhance our entire sense of wellbeing.

Try focusing on the heart center with an attitude of gratitude tonight when you do your yoga class and notice what happens. The healing power of yoga postures that clear organ or meridian blockages will be enhanced. Chi, or life force, is increased when you do the yoga poses with mindful awareness, with focus on the heart center, and a grateful attitude. You stay more present, too.

So, this is the experiment for today: whatever you're doing, stay present with it and function from a loving, grateful heart; observe the effects and notice the power of using this approach with everything. Staying heart-centered and present when you're with others will help you listen with your heart. You will be less reactive from your ego, and you will serve others in a much more powerful way. Yes, doing deep breathing from the heart center with a grateful attitude expands our being and lightens us.

[Another example of my teacher's immediate answer to my unspoken wondering about whether the expansive, light feeling I'm experiencing right now is related to the heart-focused breathing I've been doing as I write.]

It allows us to be present to the joy of the moment. Use the heart focus with a grateful attitude as much as you can throughout your day. Let this be the last thing you do before sleep and the first thing you do on waking. Notice the effects of this on your physical wellbeing, your mental and emotional state, and your spiritual connection. *[At the end of this lesson, but still as part of the lesson, my inner teacher directs me to practice breathing from the heart center with a feeling of gratitude right now. After I've stopped writing and done this for a while, she mentally places one of her hands on my heart as we breathe together and after a while places her other hand to the base of my brain. I notice feeling calmer and my breathing slows. What a wonderful experiential exercise from which to end today's lesson.]*

Personal Reflections

Today's theme centered on the importance of being in and functioning from the heart center with an attitude of gratitude in everything we do. This enhances healing and allows us to be fully present to each moment. It increases the power of whatever help we offer self or others.

My teacher is using things I know to illustrate ways to practice daily skills to enhance my learning and growth. The specific exercise she taught me of deep breathing from the heart center with an attitude of gratitude while placing one hand on my heart and the other at the base of my brain is easy to duplicate on your own with no equipment needed. I find it calming and centering. My speculation is that it's a way of connecting head-mind-heart to reduce the tendency to intellectualize or be in my head too much. The latter is often associated with worry and looking ahead, both of which deplete my energy and take me away from being fully present in the moment. Staying centered in my heart will likely increase the openness of my heart-mind-spirit to my inner teacher. The challenge will be to make routine the head-mind-heart exercise and remain heart-gratitude focused throughout the day. For me, practicing this at specific times during the day is a way to build in this new habit.

I tried the mindful heart and gratitude focus during my yoga class tonight, as my teacher suggested. I noticed I was present to each moment, centered, calmer, and less conscious of time. The yoga movements felt like a worshipful meditation in motion. Currently, I continue to reap the same benefits as I use this mindful, heart-focused approach when I practice yoga or other movement exercise. The heart-center focus with deep breathing is a helpful calming tool that can be used anytime. It also helps shift negative emotional reactions to a more neutral, less reactive response.

Today's lesson was reminiscent of the Institute of HeartMath's research and heart-focused tools for managing stress and negative emotions outlined by Childre and Martin in *The HeartMath Solution*. I have used their tools both personally and professionally with benefit. Like everything, regular practice and integration of the tools into daily life is essential.

The placement of one hand on the heart and the other at the base of the brain while using the heart-focused gratitude breathing was new to me. At the time, I knew nothing about Reiki healing touch and was unfamiliar with the hand positions used in this form of healing touch. In one of those synchronous events, I was introduced to Reiki healing touch by a friend in 2009 and subsequently completed my training in 2010. I now recognize that these hand positions relate to healing and restoring balance to the energy centers or chakras that make up the subtle energy body. Since then, practicing Reiki healing touch has become one of my most consistent reminders to remain open-hearted and grateful.

LESSON FIVE

Gratitude Touches the Spirit of Oneness in all Life

Preparatory Steps for Intuitive Journaling

<u>Meditate or center</u>

<u>Enter date and time in journal</u>

<u>Write out intention in journal</u>: intention set for pure, clear, accurate connection and communication with highest wisdom regarding whatever is most needed at this time followed by any specific concerns or questions for which you are requesting help

<u>Repeat prayer of protection</u>: As I open my heart, mind, and spirit to the unseen Divine forces around the throne of grace, mercy, and might, I am surrounded by the pure light of protection found in the thought of the Christ Consciousness.

<u>Begin writing using starter phrase</u>: If my soul or higher Self spoke to me now, and continue writing whatever comes to mind until it stops.

10/25/2006, 7:30 a.m., Lesson Five

I am here. Yes, the dawning of the day is indeed a beautiful and awe inspiring event—and it's free! *[This was said in such a lighthearted way, I laughed aloud. It acknowledged my feelings of awe for the constant beauty of nature.]*

The predictability and certainty of the daylight's dawning provides a sense of security, stability, and reliance on the laws of the universe. The daily rising and setting of the sun are so persistently consistent that you take it for granted and seldom reflect on how awesome and marvelous it is to have a universe so reliable in its ongoing service to all life and its Source. Sun's light and moon's reflected light in the darkness of night are part of the universal consciousness you call God. All things are infused with the Creator's consciousness.

When you think of daylight, the sun rising and setting, the earth and ground surface, its minerals and rocks, wind, water, and foliage in this way, you are acknowledging the oneness in all things. This noticing of nature's rhythms, cycles, and resources is another form of worship of our Source because it reflects awareness of the Divine presence in all things.

This is the key to peace, love, compassion, and understanding: to see others as reflections of self and to see the light of infinite Divinity within all things. This awareness leads to care of all living things because of the knowledge of our oneness in spirit. The desire to care for self, others, and the environment then become <u>one and the same</u> [teacher's emphasis]. Peace and living with others in peace, cooperation, sharing, compassion, and justice all begin with self and move outward to your relationships with others and your environment. If you cannot love and accept yourself as you are while you continue to work on developing spiritually and manifesting spirit's love in your daily life, then you are limited in doing that with others.

True love of self is love of your Creator and the desire to reflect the spirit of God consciousness, which is unconditional love, in your daily lives. This becomes worship of your Source because it is a concrete way you reflect praise and glory. This encompasses everything—the food you eat and how you grow it; how you care for the soil that supports life here; what you do; who you spend time with; the quality of your effort in all your activities and endeavors; and especially in your care of children, those with special needs, and all living things.

The worshipful feeling that arises when you view all of life, including today's sunlight, as manifestations of the Universal Mind is strongest in the heart center, the center for love, compassion, and oneness. That's why focusing on the heart center with feelings of loving gratitude is so powerful. It's a uniting force or at least gives you the opportunity to touch the oneness and expansiveness associated with feelings of altruistic love. It's a way to connect with your soul and the spirit of oneness in all things. As such, it is the way back to your connection with Source.

Even glimmers of this connection with All That Is result in heartfelt joy, peace, centeredness, and love. Fear melts away when you're in that place. The exercise I suggested yesterday helps with letting go of fear and reconnecting with Source. *[Deep breathing while focusing on the heart center and feelings of gratitude, with one hand on your heart and the other at the base of the brain.]*

Continue to work on the heart focus until it becomes easier to remember and maintain.

That's enough for today.

Personal Reflections

Letting each lesson unfold comes more easily now, and I am curious to see what will emerge. I try less often to control or structure the process to fit some preconceived mold. I am still curious about my inner teacher and the source of these lessons, but I am more accepting of her disclosing this, or not, as she sees fit. My focusing on the questions of who she is and how she knows things would likely interfere with my openness to receiving the lessons.

Based on yesterday's lesson, I am trying to remember to practice the heart exercise and maintain heart focus throughout the day as much as possible. I can definitely see the difference. When I am acting without heart focus, my mind and energy are scattered; there is a quality of inner tension and pressure associated with the task at hand. When I notice the tension and shift into an open-hearted focus and breathe into and out of the heart's gratitude, the effect is relaxing and my focus is clearer, sharper.

Since learning Reiki healing touch, I easily remember to combine the heart and base of brain hand positions with the heart-focused deep breathing. In addition to being deeply calming and centering, it helps release fear and reconnects me with my higher Self. Fear closes the heart and leaves me feeling separate. Opening the heart, however, is a uniting and expansive experience that restores connection to the oneness of the higher Self and universal consciousness.

As a reminder, the lessons that follow will no longer include the routine preparatory steps for intuitive journaling.

LESSON SIX

Ways to Connect with the World of Spirit

10/26/2006, 10 a.m., Lesson Six

The snow is falling. The cover of moisture-laden clouds limits your vision. This physical weather is a metaphoric description of the veil that separates the physical and spiritual dimensions of existence. The slowness of your vibrational energy in dense physical matter creates the veil and inability to see the simultaneously existing spirit dimension which is at a faster, higher vibration.

Meditation and the experiential knowing of universal consciousness allow you to become intuitively aware and to connect with your soul and the spirit dimension. The strength of the intuitive experience fosters strong belief and awareness that you are indeed more than your physical body. In those moments of expanded awareness, the veil separating the physical and spirit dimensions is lowered to give a glimpse of the world of spirit. The feelings of peace, centeredness, expansion, and love that accompany this experience spur growth. It is much like the weather-laden clouds that clear and disperse after a storm—once again you can see farther and more clearly. The more you practice seeing the spirit world, the easier it becomes to see it. Soon it is as clear as earth after a storm.

There are many ways to connect with the spiritual dimension—regular meditation, prayer, use of thoughts and mental images, and this written exercise. These all help you open to something greater than self. *[For me, one of the best ways to connect with the spiritual dimension is this intuitive journaling exercise I do each day following meditation. I set an intention for help from the highest source of wisdom then surround myself with protection. As long as I maintain an attitude of openness of heart-mind-spirit—without preconceived notions—I find the connection gives just what I need at that moment. It may be a new way of handling difficult situations or relationships; increased awareness of recurring issues I need to face and change; a sense of being loved in a way that I can find no words to describe; a clearer understanding of spiritual ideas that before were just complicated concepts; or practical ways to connect with my higher Self at any time.]*

Your state of mind and possible reluctance to openness color the information and can bring in distortions or inaccuracies. You can assess the accuracy for yourself and what works for you from these teachings. This principle of trying out or experimenting with the teachings, then observing the effects for yourself, is a general guiding principle for everything.

31

It's important not to simply accept things blindly without trying them out for yourself. Observe whether the effects are positive, free of harm, and enhance growth or, on the other hand, negative, harmful, and interfere with growth. "By their fruits shall you know them" (*The Bible, King James Version, Matthew 7.20)*: if the effects are positive, uplifting, do not cause harm, help you grow and become a better person, and increase your awareness of your soul and Source, then stay with it; you're on the right path.

To increase your awareness of and intuitive communication with the spiritual dimension, continue to learn and develop yourself in whatever constructive form works for you. Then apply what you're learning as an experiment, as noted before, with the goal of integrating those things that foster growth. Other ways to connect with the spiritual world include attention to dreams; creative expression as in art and poetry; studying esoteric readings and the teachings of enlightened beings; developing your intuition; being close to nature and increasing your awareness of the oneness of all things in spirit; applying the concepts of brotherhood in spirit and living in a way that is true to your spiritual ideals; asking for assistance from your helpers in spirit which acknowledges and uses the connection between your soul and the world of spirit; and generally seeking to learn more about the spiritual dimension, then applying the resulting knowledge and wisdom to your everyday physical life.

This is, after all, the purpose of manifestation in physical form: to remember you are spirit in physical form whose task is to learn from your life experiences and return to your connection with Source; and to realize your true Self, spirit created by Source, by manifesting this universal love and returning to your natural state of oneness with Source.

Even as visibility is poor and limited with the physical snowstorm you are now experiencing and the sun is still present even though it can't be seen, so too spirit and the work of spirit are always present and ongoing even when you are in physical form and may be unaware of your soul and the spiritual dimension.

We are always here working at our tasks, listening for and responding to your requests for guidance. When you make contact with us as you have with me, we celebrate. We are elated because of the opportunity this provides for lowering the veil and communicating teachings that will enrich your life there. Thank you for seeking and allowing this communication and committing consistent time for this.

That's enough for today.

Personal Reflections

We are having a blizzard that has closed down most of the city. The dense cloud cover from the snow front has limited visibility and darkened the day as if the sun were gone. I was tickled by my inner teacher's use of the snowstorm metaphor to describe the veil between the physical world of matter and the world of spirit.

Strong doubts recurred regarding the source of this material and its benefit to others.

My inner teacher's response reminded me that the actual lessons are of greatest importance for our purposes. Readers can discern for themselves the accuracy and benefits of the teachings as applied to their own lives. My inner teacher's encouragement to test the effects of the teachings for one's self and to keep what is helpful seemed sensible. In response to my doubts regarding the value of this material, I decided to remain positive and open to the lessons. I will test them out whenever possible and focus on doing my best to accurately receive and record the lessons. As for my doubts about whether others will benefit from these lessons, I decided to leave that where it rightly belongs, in the hands of readers to assess for themselves.

My inner teacher assured me this internal source of wisdom is accessible at any time. She encouraged me to maintain mental openness to this inner wisdom throughout the day to begin building the habit of using it whenever I need it. This is very challenging. I often forget or am unable to sustain the kind of open, focused awareness I need in the midst of the usual stuff of daily life. When I am able to be open to and tap in to this inner guidance during the day's events, even in small ways, it is always enlightening. I notice more synchronous events—meaningful coincidences—that provide what is needed in a seemingly effortless way. I keep reminding myself to remain persistent in practicing connecting with inner guidance throughout the day.

There are many good books and workshops on developing intuition. A few of these include Barbara Brennan's *Hands of*

Light; Shakti Gawain's *Living in the Light Workbook;* Barbara Marx Hubbard's *Emergence;* Caroline Myss and C. Norman Shealy's workshops on intuition; Belleruth Naparstek's *Your Sixth Sense;* Christel Nani's *Guidance 24/7* and *Diary of a Medical Intuitive;* Judith Orloff's workshops; Judith Pennington's *Your Psychic Soul* and her guided meditation CDs; Henry Reed's *Channeling Your Higher Self,* using Edgar Cayce's concepts; Mona Lisa Schulz's *Awakening Intuition;* James Van Praagh's *Heaven and Earth* and workshops on intuition; and Doreen Virtue's *Divine Guidance* and *Divine Prescriptions.*

LESSON SEVEN

Let Go of Effort and Control

10/27/06, 7:30 a.m., Lesson Seven

Your excessive effort clouds things and interferes with your hearing me. Remember to simply be open to receiving. This is good practice for you as you try too hard at many things, not trusting the process will unfold as it should and that you will be ready to handle it. Your struggle and self-criticalness during meditation is also an impediment. Simply relax around the process and let go of striving to get quiet because the struggle for control that ensues is not helpful.

Remember what you teach patients: acknowledge the negative feeling or thought without reacting to it or trying to push it away; simply observe its presence with an attitude of detachment, then let it go. After all, you are not the negative thought, feeling, or distraction. It's the nature of the mind to wander and the ego to control. Even though you teach these things to your patients, seeing these tendencies in self is more difficult. Integrating what you teach others becomes more difficult due to these blind spots. That's where I can be helpful by pointing out your forced effort with me. It interferes. Opening to receiving or listening is much harder than it sounds.

It's a human habit to analyze or try to control what enters the mind's awareness. Noticing thoughts, the desire to control them, your judgments, or discouragement in response to these distractions are all part of the process in meditation. A meditative life is one of noticing and releasing all the distractions in order to come to the place of stillness within that connects you with something greater that is not Self yet is part of Self. It is what you call your Source or All That Is. Yes, in response to your mental question about whether you heard the phrasing of my thought accurately, "come to" was the correct phrase rather than find as you were thinking because find implies effort and control. When you experience the inner stillness even for a brief moment, it's an unforgettable experience. Because you desire more of this peaceful, expansive feeling, you work or effort to bring it back or find it again. So there you are once more trying to control your experience. Instead, move with the flow; notice distractions, release them without judgment, attachment, or attempts to suppress them.

Stillness is always present within you. It is not necessary to try to find it. It is only necessary to trust that it is eternally present. This is, after all, your connection with your soul and spirit of oneness with all, your spark of the Divine which doesn't ever leave or hide from you. Trust your awareness of its presence within and in all things. *[As my teacher says this, I realize I have often mistakenly felt my connection with spirit was hidden from me or out of my reach because I thought I had to work hard to connect with it. Only after beginning a consistent meditation practice did I get glimpses of its inner stillness and peacefulness. It was then I began to understand that my trying-hard attitude could be replaced with one of openness and allowing. I had to get my ego self out of the way to connect with the stillness of the higher Self which is always present. I had to stop trying to control and direct it, and simply be with the experience.]*

Stay with the process of noticing. Observe what distracts you from sitting with and in the stillness. Release any distractions without force, criticism, or judgment. If you persist in this practice of simply observing and your intention is to touch the stillness in this way, it will in fact happen when you are ready. It's necessary to learn to let go of effort and control—notice it and release it. Replace it with acceptance of what is present. Know that this is the way to stillness within and to connection with the Source of All That Is.

How can something that sounds so simple be so difficult? *[My teacher voices my exact thoughts.]* Persist with the process; this is what needs to be learned and practiced. Attachment to wanting more of anything, including the experience of touching stillness, involves effort and control. Relinquish these attitudes and you will experience stillness. Yes, it's a paradox and contrary to the way much of your physical life is lived. Your persistence is an indication of the sincerity of your intention. You want to be consciously aware of living from spirit.

That's enough for today.

Personal Reflections

I reread this particular lesson after I finished and smiled as I recognized the accuracy of observations about how much of my behavior is about trying hard, directing, and controlling. This tendency to approach life as something to be managed or controlled is a strong conditioned response for me and, I suspect, for most people.

The ongoing work of this journaling is noticing, observing, and letting go without judgment or attachment. I recognize how easy it is to get strongly attached to the deep feeling of peace and expansiveness associated with the inner experience of stillness during meditation and intuitive journaling. The message seems to be to notice and let go of this attachment as well as striving to get or stay there. If I don't let go, it interferes with the experience of touching the stillness within me. I have a long way to go, I think, then realize I have just slipped into effort and judgment again. Another moment to practice noticing and releasing, staying with an attitude of acceptance in the present moment.

LESSON EIGHT

All Living Things Are One

10/28/06, 4:40 p.m., Lesson Eight

This gorgeous fall day is alive with beauty and energy. All you see and admire of nature from here is alive. It is part of universal consciousness.

You are each one with all living things. They are created, like you, by the Source of All That Is. The beauty and growth of nature is there for you to enjoy and use. Your part is to appreciate and care for it properly. All things are interdependent in this way. Each person's part within the whole is needed to create and maintain balance and harmony in nature as well as within your individual and collective lives. *[Shakti Gawain in <u>Reflections in the Light</u> presents an interesting perspective related to this. She suggests that earth symbolizes our collective body and that Mother Nature symbolizes the nurturing, intuitive aspect of ourselves. So, the way we treat earth and our natural environment mirrors the* *way we treat our bodies. To me, this implies that the extent to which we globally disregard our natural environment reflects the extent of our own lack of harmonious attunement with our physical bodies which are spirit in physical matter. On the flip side, healthy awareness of and alignment with our intuitive, soul nature and the nurturance of our physical bodies cannot help but reflect itself in a more balanced, healthy treatment of our planet. I like this perspective. It's empowering and brings home the oneness and interdependence of all life in a powerfully uplifting way.]*

If you take nature for granted and arrogantly see the natural environment as there to enjoy and use with no responsibility for wise use on your part, you are approaching the natural world in a mindless, unaware state that will ultimately create damage. When you approach creation unaware, with lack of consciousness of the connection and mutual responsibility of all things, there will be no peace, harmony, balance, or right use. Although nature, its food, and animals are present for your enjoyment, sustenance, and health, they too are evolving, and their development and wellbeing depend on the quality of care you give them. Your growth and development are dependent on the care you direct toward yourself and others as well as your environment, planet, and galaxy. This theme of interdependence is present throughout the human and natural world.

Right action toward others and your planetary environment affects all of you and your development in a positive way. Likewise, negative behavior toward others and your planet negatively impact all of you. For example, the quality of the air, water, soil, and food and the hardiness of trees, animals, farm crops, and wildlife are all affected for good or bad by your individual and collective choices.

This earth is your collective home. Caring for it is the responsibility of each of you. The wisdom with which you do so affects your quality of life and, in some cases, whether you live or die. Polluting the earth creates health problems and disease for humans and the earth. The earth is a living entity as are all the varieties of plant, sea, and animal life sustained by earth's resources. This is a call to awaken to awareness of the aliveness and oneness of all creation, both human and the natural world.

It is good to express gratitude to all of nature for its beauty and its life-giving gifts of air, sunlight, water, soil for growing food, and raw materials for your creations and needs.

Earth is alive and affected by your actions. That is the law of cause and effect that governs all things.

Thank you for dedicating your yoga practice to me this morning and remembering to stay heart-focused. You're beginning to think of and connect with me at times other than our daily writing meetings. That is good, and as it should be, since I am always present and available to assist you.

That's enough for today.

Personal Reflections

I continue to notice that the intuitive writing flows more easily in the morning versus afternoons or evenings. It seems the cumulative stress of the day interferes with maintaining clear mental focus and a receptive attitude. As a result, if I try to write at night, the connection with my inner teacher seems less solid, and the flow of the lesson does not come as easily. Aside from this observation, whenever I do the intuitive journaling the lessons typically last from twenty to thirty minutes.

Continuing to transcribe what my inner teacher communicates despite my frequent attacks of doubt reflects my underlying belief in this process and my commitment to sharing the lessons. You, reader, will decide for yourself whether it is beneficial for you. My inner teacher assures me there is nothing unique about what I am doing. Anyone can do this if he or she is willing and open. Most of us are inclined to dismiss these experiences as impossible. We think it's either a figment of our imagination or we doubt its validity. Yet the world of spirit, though invisible to us, is as present and alive as our physical world. Since its vibrational energy permeates everything, our being able to access it is a matter of readiness, willingness, belief in its possibility, and commitment to doing the work.

Acknowledging the aliveness of our natural environment and our interdependence with it is a good place to start practicing gratitude and wise care for the endless beauty, life-giving bounty, and constant replenishment of our earth. If you talk with people who love plants or pets, many will tell you they talk with them in encouraging, appreciative ways, noticing their struggles, challenges, and strengths just as we might in human interactions. They may even admit to lovingly talking with and preparing their plants for pruning and transplanting and their pets for inoculations or surgery much as we might prepare children or loved ones for stressful times and events. Others make a point of using meditative walks or hikes to mindfully notice and appreciate the natural beauty all around.

So, don't be shy about admiring and appreciating every aspect of the natural world, silently or aloud, whether you're driving, biking, getting the newspaper, gardening, weeding, or looking out your window. Notice the unique beauty and quirks of wildlife and domesticated pets, the sound of birds singing, or animals rustling in leaves and shrubs. Notice the vast array of colors, the feel of the sun, the fragrance of flowers and the air after a rainstorm, the inspiring radiance of rainbows, the constant change in cloud patterns and shadows. Touch, talk to a tree; notice how unique each tree is.

One of my favorite practices is use of Thich Naht Hahn's conscious breathing exercise. It is simple and can be adapted to any circumstance. For example, when I'm walking outdoors, I silently repeat some variation of the following in rhythm with my breath: breathing in, I breathe in the life-giving air around me; breathing out, I breathe out gratitude for this air that sustains me. Or, I breathe in the beauty around me; I breathe out gratitude for nature's gift of beauty. Better yet, create one that fits you and notice any changes in your attitudes and feelings toward yourself, nature, and others as you practice it. As my attitude shifts, my awareness of and care for our natural environment as a living thing also expands.

LESSON NINE

Lighten Up

10/29/06, 11:30 a.m., Lesson Nine

You continue to make your preparation for this more difficult than it needs to be. Your perfectionist approach reflects underlying, incorrect fears of creating a mess from not doing it right. It's time to let go of that black and white way of viewing your behavior. It's alright and much more enjoyable to have a sense of lightness about yourself and to trust your intentions as well as our care for you. *[Now there's a new, more positive way of approaching life! What a relief to let go of that false sense of control—it's heavy, burdensome, all self-imposed. I'm struck again by the amount of misery I can create with negative thinking. I definitely feel happy and free when connected with this inner sense of lightness about self and life.]*

There are no perfect ways to do things, only different ways that mirror the uniqueness of each person and where they are in their own evolution. You're all on the same road, headed toward the same destination of returning to join with your Source. The ways of getting there are varied and there is no right or perfect way. Detours taken along the way are possible due to free will. They are opportunities for growth and learning, depending on how they're viewed and used. Helping fellow travelers is a part of the journey. Willingness to do so out of genuine desire to be helpful brings you closer to your Source. It allows others this opportunity too if they are wise users of help and assistance in their journey.

The speed of the journey is relatively unimportant since there is no time here in the world of spirit. *[This is difficult to wrap my mind around, as time is part of our physical reality and is even necessary for running our world. Our preoccupation with and rush to do more, faster seems unhealthy. We often act as if time controls us rather than our being in charge of how we use time. I remember enjoying the response of a mindfulness workshop teacher to a question about how to handle rush and hurry in our everyday world: she told us to try to focus on one thing at a time and, if you have to hurry, do it mindfully, with full attention. Perhaps the attitude with which we approach and respond to time in physical life is most important. For instance, we can prioritize the type and number of activities we participate in throughout the day. We can focus our attention mindfully on whatever we've chosen to do, concentrating on the quality and enjoyment instead of the speed with which we complete it. When I remember to do this, I've discovered my work not only gets done but I relax and enjoy even mundane tasks. We always have control over our attitude toward time and the things we've chosen to do with our time. So, approaching our time-based life as one centered on how we use time rather than speed may be a way of assimilating the timeless attitude of spirit into our physical life experiences.]*

How you think, behave, and act during your journey is extremely important. Of major import are: thoughts of gratitude and appreciation; thoughts and actions that consider others along with self; delight in the views and experiences along the way; clear focus on the goal of reuniting with your Source; making choices and decisions that lead toward this goal; and seeing all experiences, including hardships, as learning experiences to move you toward reuniting with All That Is. Caring for other humans, animals, and your natural environment along the way is the attitude that reflects your awareness in action that all is one. All things are animated by the infinite light or energy of the Creator's love and life source. This active caring gives you a new appreciation for all of life. See all things through your new eyes—sense, feel the vibration of oneness within all things.

Yes, in response to your thoughts, you are correct in noting the challenge of seeing this oneness and the Divine spark in humans when they act in negative, harmful ways. *[My mental question was actually a judgment as it's hard for me, and most others, to see the divine light in myself and others when we act in destructive ways.]* Such behavior only reflects the choice from ignorance or free will to disregard the light within. The choice to remain in darkness by refusing to examine self and the effects your behaviors have on others is mistakenly associating your control over others as power.

True power comes from self-reflection and acknowledging responsibility for your thoughts, feelings, behavior, and actions as well as their effects on self and others. True power is rooted in making choices that lead you to reuniting with Source, the universal light and love. Following the guidance of the Divine light that resides within all living things is up to each human. It necessarily requires the exercise of free will. The true purpose of life, to manifest the universal light of love, is a choice available to all.

That's enough for today.

Personal Reflections

I'm getting many reminders and opportunities to practice trusting the intuitive writing process. It's clear I need to learn to let go of trying too hard to get it perfect. I'm receiving unexpected help identifying my beliefs that I can control negative events and outcomes through effort and doing everything right. This misguided belief that I can control the results of negative events through sheer effort diminishes when I deliberately reframe my thoughts to ones that are more reasonable, objective, and positive. I notice that my reframed thought is what I have taught patients: I, like every other human being, am only responsible for and in charge of my own thoughts, feelings, behavior, and actions; like others, I am imperfect; I will consistently persist in doing my best.

I am beginning to understand that the issue of importance is not control but keeping an open heart-mind to the light of spirit within and doing my best to act from this.

Despite these optimistic glimmers, ongoing doubts and fears keep showing up in the lessons that follow. I've included this repetition for two reasons. First, to give you an accurate picture of the persistence required by all of us in the process of changing entrenched, distorted, or negative patterns in our thinking, feelings, and beliefs. Second, it shows the layered, cyclic nature of the learning path for all personal and soul growth. I think of this as uncovering an infinite number of onion layers. The outermost layer represents the issues currently present for our attention and learning. Rarely are we one trial learners. Most often, lessons to be learned surface repeatedly in a variety of ways and at different levels to help us assimilate and integrate what needs to be mastered. Signs of progress and challenges are noticeable at every layer of work. When we have actively engaged our current lessons and sufficiently progressed, the next layer of those lessons will emerge to facilitate ongoing development. This is cause for celebration as it reflects positive momentum in our spiritual evolution. Most of us recognize this repeating, layered aspect of learning when we encounter a lesson in forgiving someone, for example, years after we thought we had put it to rest. Looking closely, we can usually see a deeper meaning to forgiveness of which we were unaware or new opportunities to extend forgiveness. The point is to patiently persist in assimilating and practicing the unique soul growth lessons that accompany our current level of development.

Resistance to change is common and frequently is our initial fearful response to something unfamiliar. Being willing to acknowledge our negative reactions to change and looking honestly at the fears underneath our resistance is useful. It helps us clarify our pattern of response to change and evaluate the positive and negative effects we create in a particular situation. From there, we can look at the range of options open to us and choose a response that is most constructive, moving ourselves out of resistance into adaptation to change and growth.

LESSON
TEN

Accept and Reframe Negative Thoughts

10/30/06, 7:30 a.m., Lesson Ten

Let go of your anxiety about doing a good job with this journal. It will lighten your load. It will help you let go of expectations of a certain outcome. You will feel free and light. You can then enjoy this process and look forward to it with curiosity and anticipation.

For years you strengthened a conditioned response to steel yourself to deal with each new day and its events. This left you with a sense of dread toward your day and all it offered. Your intuitive insight about this a few years ago allowed you to begin changing this negative conditioned response to one where you looked forward to each day and its experiences. You became confident you would manage whatever came up. *[My teacher is reminding me of an unforgettable insight experience from years ago. On waking from sleep one morning, I had a strong, clear awareness*

51

of my habit of waking up with a sense of dread about the day ahead. I could feel and almost taste the sense of apprehension in my stomach and the physical tension this created in my waking body. Unless I was able to release that with meditation or journaling, I carried that uneasiness into the day. I was aware of my strong perfectionist qualities despite years of work on their negative effects. Still, I had to laugh when I recognized the level of stress and misery I was creating for myself with my perfectionism that I carried even into sleep. I realized if I could create that level of unnecessary fear, physical tension, and stress with my mind and thoughts, I could also do the opposite. So, I resolved to reverse my old conditioned response. I did that through repeated use of this positive, empowering nighttime visualization and affirmation: My sleep will be peaceful throughout the night and deeply restorative; I'll wake easily in the morning feeling energized, refreshed, and eager to meet the new day. I still use this nighttime visualization when my stress level rises and I begin to revert to old thinking habits based in fear. I used my journaling to further understand and change the recurring negative thinking patterns that fueled my old irrational attitude of dread and fear in starting each day.]

Your approach to this writing is similar to your former habit of steeling yourself to do a good job. The stress produced by believing you have to expend great effort to live up to the high expectations you bring to this writing is yet another layer of the negative tension and dread you woke with and carried into your day for so many years. Our journaling is continuing that work of letting go of tension, apprehensive effort, outcome, and perfectionist expectations. Trust the process of life to serve up lessons needed. Build confidence in your ability to deal with whatever arises while remembering we are always here to support you. Remember, too, that what happens is often positive, not negative, as you fear.

Steeling yourself against anticipated difficulties is not a helpful or adaptive attitude. It's fear-based behavior. Replace the fear with its opposite: trust you will lovingly face and learn from whatever is present in your daily life.

Your negative reaction to the windy weather today is an immediate opportunity to practice this. Examine your pattern of resisting what is and labeling it negative or unpleasant. Notice your judgments attached to the windy weather, the negative feelings associated with your evaluation, your resistance to accepting its presence. Replace your negative judgment with a balanced perspective. For example, notice how the wind bends the trees and sways the golden aspen leaves. Allow this opportunity to appreciate nature's beauty as it moves with wind and captures your attention. Think of the wind clearing out debris physically, mentally, and emotionally in a figurative way. You can visualize the wind moving out old, stuck energy to make room for revitalized energy. This visualization allows you to think and feel differently, choosing to focus on the positive aspects of wind.

This is good training in changing negative conditioned responses. They serve no constructive purpose and need to be replaced with empowering responses. These are the same skills you taught patients for managing and changing negative emotions like depression, anxiety, fears, panic, anger, and frustration. Thoughts are energy and, as such, are real and powerful in their effects.

You have correctly used those concepts to reframe your upcoming retirement to life transition from a career as a clinical psychologist to other types of work that are equally meaningful. One's life purpose of serving and helping can be done in a multitude of ways. It's society that labels and values some as better than others. This is a mistake. It is an example of a culturally conditioned response that is inaccurate. Anything that diminishes the value of yourself or others is a judgment.

Let today's windy weather clear out the cobwebs of the mind and body, allowing room for new energy and growth. This fits with the preparatory work for your life transition from career to other vocations that may or may not be paid. Some kinds of work have the potential to generate income and then you have the exciting task of deciding how to use the income generated. *[I find my unpaid volunteer work, such as Reiki healing touch, as satisfying, rewarding, and fun as deciding how to use income from paid work.]*

That's enough for today. Enjoy the wind of nature. Allow it to blow out the old and blow in the new. *[She said this with such humor that laughter seemed the only natural response. I came away from this lesson with lightness and hope.]*

Personal Reflections

I continue to be delighted and surprised by the free-form process of this writing, the unpredictability of the topics, and the humor of my teacher. I had great resistance to journaling today but am glad I did not give in to the anxiety or the desire to avoid it. I now feel lighter; the anxiety has vanished. I benefited greatly from my teacher's insights. I got a kick out of her using the same concepts of reframing negative thoughts that I have used in therapy with patients and in my own personal work.

On my drive to work, I stayed present and enjoyed nature along the way instead of letting my mind wander.

Though I thought I was doing a pretty decent job of integrating the skills that I teach patients into my own life, my teacher today revealed a whole other layer of this work of which I was unaware. The humor with which my teacher points out things needing my personal work makes it very easy to hear and acknowledge. There's no blame, criticism, or judgment. Simply a sincere desire to help me and others grow. I hope I mirror this attitude with my patients as well as my teacher does with me.

As I prepare patients for my leaving and transition those who need ongoing treatment to other psychologists, I realize I am helping them deal with their feelings about a major change which they did not initiate. They have no control over my leaving but must adapt to it. It's also a part of my preparation for my own major life transition. Working through the range of normal feelings that go with this unexpected change and loss—sadness, anxiety, anger, feeling abandoned, accepting what cannot be controlled— has been emotionally intense for my patients and me.

LESSON
ELEVEN

Facing What We Fear

10/31/06, 7:30 a.m., Lesson Eleven

I see that you still experience anxiety in anticipation of this work. This anxious part of you wants to resist and avoid writing. Thank you for not giving in to the fearful urge to avoid your journaling. As you've taught patients, facing what you're anxious about is the healthiest way to master fears. That, as you know, is when you actually learn and grow from fear.

Never has there been a more powerful teacher than fear. It provides repeated opportunities to face and learn from the fear or to persist with avoidance, which thoroughly disempowers you.

The stillness of this cold, overcast day with its low overhanging clouds and bits of snow like a white transparent curtain in the mild wind is quite a contrast to yesterday's blustery, warm day. Both can be used as metaphors to examine fear and anxiety. Yesterday's winds bear a resemblance to how you allow yourselves to be blown this way and that by fears and anxieties, never still long enough to examine the fears up close to see what they're about. In your mindlessness, you give in to the fears which then buffet and bend you every which way. Out of habit, you are afraid to stand still and face your fears. You are afraid to try something different than avoidance.

Today's stillness and the barely perceptible creeping of the gray-white fog on the ground are reminiscent of what happens when you still your body-mind and stand to face your fears. If you can come to understand what your fears are telling you and what's needed to allow the anxiety to disperse and lighten like thin, foggy clouds dispelled by the gentle wind, you become strong, you learn something about yourself.

Standing your ground to face fears with curiosity and trust that they have essential information to teach for your growth is, after all, what allows you to see the true nature of your fears. To look underneath them and pull out what's been buried can release the fear. You become transformed, lighter for having used your courage to face it. As with today's weather, the sun is still present and shedding light even though it's not clearly visible.

In facing your anxiety about this work yet again today, you have discovered that your fears were groundless. Something of import always arises from heartfelt intention and genuine effort. Your fears simply reflect a mistaken attitude of separateness where everything is up to you, leading once again to effort and anxiety about failing to produce a satisfactory outcome, whatever that is.

Perhaps using the transformative breath exercise you've taught patients would help you release the distorted fears about this daily work: using diaphragmatic breathing, breathe in the fear where you experience it in your body and release it with each outbreath, forcing nothing. An alternative would be to breathe in the fear and breathe out the opposite feeling (in this case, calm and relaxed curiosity), again with no effort, no force. Another option would be to simply sit with and observe the fear without judging or trying to change it, trusting this process to reveal the fallacies behind your fear so they can be released.

One of your underlying fears is that of messing up, not being good enough, being judged or ridiculed. Remember what you teach patients with similar distorted beliefs about the importance of pleasing others: it's most essential to do your best at being true to and accepting of who and what you are, with no apologies, since you alone are responsible and accountable for your own life choices, just as others are responsible and accountable for theirs. Others' approval is not a requirement for happiness and growth. Being who and what you are as unique, one-of-a-kind individuals is what you each bring to the greater good and your own spiritual development. It is your contribution to the universal light that no one else can provide.

Social and cultural conditioning throughout the years, especially for women, has incorrectly taught and rewarded compliance, deferring to, and pleasing others as the basis for self-worth. This conditioning is fear based and a misuse of power. It is another attempt to control others through judgment and manipulation to meet one's own needs and expectations. Yes, of course, women behave incorrectly in this way too and men have also been unfairly trained through social and cultural conditioning to hide feelings mistakenly labeled as weak and unmanly. The task of both genders is to become more aware of the limiting, growth-interfering effects of negative conditioning and to change these false internalized beliefs so all can fully realize who and what they are and express their unique purposes in the world.

That's enough for today.

Personal Reflections

As usual, facing today's uncertainty about writing and doing it anyway eliminated my irrational anxiety. Seeing the writing flow easily pointed out the flawed thinking underneath my self-doubt. I keep wondering if connecting with my highest spiritual wisdom is really this easy—show up for work consistently, state my intention, open my heart-mind-spirit, write it down. It's an awesome discovery and flies in the face of limiting beliefs we hold: that access to the world of spirit is nonexistent while we are in physical form; that it's very difficult and can be done by only a few individuals with special gifts; and it's unscientific if not downright weird.

The key, I think, is my response to the experiences that arise from this connection with the spiritual plane. Do I dismiss or ignore these experiences? Do I avoid them out of fear of the unknown? Am I willing to open to them as learning opportunities while staying firmly grounded? Can I clearly evaluate and test the effects? Am I willing to choose to benefit from helpful lessons that produce constructive change and cause no harm?

I am enjoying my inner teacher's use of weather as metaphor since metaphor does not come naturally to me. Seeing through my teacher's eyes today's gray foggy clouds moving with the wind made me understand metaphor and my anxious feelings. And then when the clouds were blown away and dispersed into nothingness, it represented in such a simple but graphic way my own process of facing, accepting, then releasing my doubts.

The experience of intuitive journaling is truly interactive on a mental and emotional level. My inner teacher never fails to respond to my unspoken thoughts and feelings.

The transformative breath exercise described in this lesson can be used throughout the day to release and change negative emotions. I use it this way regularly and always benefit. As you notice the negative emotion and what it's connected to, shift into deep breathing from the abdomen. The idea is to breathe in the negative emotion wherever you feel it in your body with an attitude of nonjudgment with each inhalation and, with each exhalation, allow the painful emotion to release. Doing this in an open-hearted way where you allow yourself to be compassionately present with the discomfort of the unwanted feeling helps you learn to be less fearful of it. It allows the negative emotion to dissolve. It also builds in the new habit of awareness of unwanted emotions, what they're connected to, and empowering yourself to face and release them, using the breath and open-hearted intention to detach from energy depleting emotions.

LESSON
TWELVE

Beginning to Face our own Darkness

11/1/06, 7:30 a.m., Lesson Twelve

The stillness is present again today as you look out and admire the breathtaking scenery—snowcapped Pikes Peak lit up by the emerging sun against an expanse of bright blue sky. You wonder what makes sunlit days so much cheerier and pleasant. Knowing the sun is there because you see evidence of it is very different from knowing the sun is there when its light is shrouded from view by storm clouds and overcast sky. Somehow, it's easier to have hope and optimism when you see visible evidence of the things in which you believe. So much of life is like that: it's easier to love or like someone whose behavior toward you reflects their love or care for you. It's easier to trust nature and see its benevolence when weather is stable and there is enough food and water than during times of floods or droughts. It's easier to believe and have hope when things are going well in your life. It's easier to have a sunny disposition when it's pleasantly sunny.

So much more difficult to love, have compassion and understanding, or forgive anyone who is spiteful, hateful, abusive, aggressive, or destructive. These behaviors provide challenge and opportunity to see the sunlight—Son's Light—in humans at their worst. *[This pun and metaphor were delivered with humor and delight.]* The desire to retaliate against such behavior in others is because of your need to deny the deep awareness that this could be any of you. Everyone is capable of acting from darkness and the desire to destroy what threatens them. You push away this awareness of your own potential to harm and destroy and, indeed, the many actual times you have behaved with harm toward others. *[I sensed my teacher's reference to harm toward others was meant in a much broader sense than physical harm and included all forms of denigrating and disrespectful words, thoughts, and behaviors.]*

It is too awful to see yourself in the mirror of other's dark actions. So you distance from it. You deny the presence of light in all things because of the fear of facing your own and others' darkness and being destroyed by it. Your faith in the light and love of universal consciousness falters at such times. It's safer to see the dark behavior of others as "not self." Otherwise, at some deeper level you would have to acknowledge this potential within yourself and the actual ways you have created harm, intentionally and unintentionally. *[These are universal lessons we all face. I still find it emotionally painful to recall times I mistreated others through unkind, blaming, and ill-tempered behavior.*

Yet I recognize, at least intellectually, that these incidents of my creating harm are also opportunities to examine what is driving my hurtful behavior and to take responsibility for correcting it. They are also lessons in directing compassion and forgiveness toward self since I am unlikely to extend genuine compassion and forgiveness to others if I am unable to do so toward myself. What I do to others, I do to myself and vice versa. It is of equal importance to direct kindness, respectful behavior, understanding, compassion, and forgiveness to self as it is to others. I just keep persisting with this moment-to-moment work of thinking, speaking, and acting from genuine care and compassion in all my relationships. The smallest of successes with this lesson are far-reaching. Each success strengthens this process of directing the power of my will to act with kindness from the higher Self, that inclusive place where we are one.]

Personal Reflections

My teacher's consideration for my work schedule today was evident in a shortened writing session to allow time to get to work without rush. This provides a wonderful role model for me of accepting and appreciating whatever others are able and willing to offer without pressuring them from my own need for something different.

The humorous pun early on in this chapter helped lighten the heaviness of this universal lesson we all face of taking responsibility for correcting the ways we cause harm—deliberately or unintentionally. The rapidness with which we revert to adverse criticism, focus on others' shortcomings, or retaliate in reaction to others' negative behavior is downright scary at times. This is especially true when the concept of harm toward others is expanded to our mental life, our thoughts. We can all relate to the experience of managing to keep our outward behavior together at times we're upset while at the same time going off on the other person in unvoiced self-righteous thoughts and perhaps later complaining bitterly to someone else about the other person as if they're to blame for our upset.

This lesson provides a more empowering way to work with the ways we cause harm: to view others as a mirror for ourselves. Seen in this light, my awareness of the small mind signs of lower nature ego desires in others is my cue to look within and discern what I need to learn from it. Since what we see in others, positive or negative, is within us, all interactions become potential healing opportunities. They might, for example, reflect unaddressed problems or recurring issues that are coming up to be healed; or even undiscovered gifts, skills, and strengths that need to be acknowledged and developed.

There's a lot to be said for focusing on and engaging with others' positive and admirable qualities in an open-hearted way in our innermost thoughts as well as our behavior, instead of reverting to critical reactions. It not only empowers us, it fosters soul growth and positive, heart-focused living. We can use our connection and alignment with the inner wisdom of our higher Self to provide the highest, most positive, and balanced guidance for the spiritual growth of our physical ego self and its small mind ways. Of course, this does not imply we need to subject ourselves to other's abusive or hurtful behavior. Self-defense when our actual physical safety is threatened is instinctual. Self-assertion is an essential, integral part of healthy self-care. It empowers us and encourages respectful ways of relating and communicating.

LESSON
THIRTEEN

Do Your Best and Let Go of the Outcome

11/2/06, 7:30 a.m., Lesson Thirteen

You are still not able to trust my instruction about the simplicity of your preparation for this. *[An observation made with humor in response to my ongoing perfectionism in beginning this intuitive communication. My teacher is referring to my carefulness in repeating the routine steps as if any mistake, such as reversing the sequence of steps, will make communication impossible. She patiently persists in helping me understand that the degree to which I repeat the preparatory steps perfectly has nothing to do with establishing our communication. Rather, it's my asking with sincerity, open-hearted listening, persisting in showing up, and detaching from the outcome that are important.]*

You'll get there at your own pace. Remember, it's not necessary to make it hard or perfect; that is not what brings me here and near to you. It's only your asking and openness to me and the teachings I offer. I'm belaboring this point because you often conclude that the degree of your effort is what brought about the outcome. There's no requirement that your effort be perfect or done in a certain way. All you need to do is ask from your heart, be ready to do your part to the best of your ability, and to persist when things don't go as you thought they would.

The inaccurate conclusion that the outcome is due to your perfect effort has created a conditioned response where you now automatically see your effort as tied to the quality of outcome. It's simpler and more humble than that. Your asking and genuinely desiring help from your heart as well as accepting that the outcome is only partly because of you and mostly from the unfolding of the universal plan that is more vast than any of us know—this is all that's needed. We—you—are one small piece of that larger plan that is always unfolding.

So my emphasis on letting go of your effort to prepare perfectly is to help you correct your mistaken notion that you are the only one in control of outcome. I am giving you the opportunity to change this. The simplest, truest way is to ask from your heart, do your part by showing up, doing your best, persisting even when things are difficult— especially when things are difficult—and then detaching from the outcome. Trust that the plan of universal love always provides the result that is best within the context of the greater plan of which you and others know next to nothing. This simpler approach will free up a great deal of energy that is wasted on excessive effort to do things perfectly.

Don't misunderstand me here. Best effort is important and your asking, initiating, and persisting are essential. It's the tension and intensity of effort that are unnecessary. It is, in fact, wasteful because it is not the determining factor in outcome. I can feel your understanding of this and your relaxing around this correction. *[For the first time, I'm beginning to grasp at a deeper level what my teacher has repeatedly tried to convey. This is another example of the layered, repetitive nature of our lessons that I referred to in Lesson nine.]*

Now, begin to implement and integrate this change in thinking. You'll get practice with this every time you begin preparation for our work sessions. Begin to be aware of other areas of your life where this incorrect attitude shows up. Often it's in situations where you are taking responsibility for things that are not yours, thinking your quality of effort and care can control others' learning or the outcome of their situations.

That's enough for today.

Personal Reflections

My inner teacher has again taken great care in this lesson to point out the core belief I have unconsciously operated from over the years that outcomes are controlled by the perfection and extent of my effort and care. My belief that I could control results through effort was so ingrained that it took a long time to grasp what she repeatedly tried to convey—that outcomes are not under my control but are guided by a universal plan beyond my knowledge or comprehension.

The care my teacher took in patiently pointing this out until I got it reflects the importance of my learning this lesson. I see now I have operated under this assumption that the degree of my effort dictates results for most of my life. This helps explain my overdeveloped sense of responsibility as well as my past habit of beginning each day with a sense of tension and dread.

What an eye-opening experience to understand this in a realistic way. My part is simply to apply the best of my abilities to those things over which I have control. Results and outcomes arise from and are guided by a greater, wiser plan and source to which I am not privy. Now that I'm more consciously aware of my old belief, I'll watch for it in the form of perfectionist effort, taking myself too seriously, or acting like I'm in charge of the universe. This writing is an ideal place to work with the lesson of letting go of results and outcome. Looking back over the last six years, I see signs of growth with this lesson. I am more aware of times I slip back into excessive effort which then becomes my cue to relax, just do my part, and let go of the outcome.

Good thing it's never too late to learn new things. I again feel the weight lifted with today's correction of this false belief from which I've lived much of my life. As I keep practicing and getting better at this, I am confident that the energy freed up from letting go of worry and trying to control outcomes will allow for greater creative expression. I'll enjoy life more, I trust, and reap the benefits of a positive productivity instead of being driven by the tension of perfectionism. Years ago, another psychologist friend and I would laughingly tease each other with the phrase "just let it go." Despite the joking context, we genuinely appreciated the importance of the concept of letting go of things not under our control. Today's lesson gave me a new level of understanding and appreciation of its importance in my life.

LESSON FOURTEEN

Oh, the Lessons to be Learned from Crankiness

11/3/06, 2:15 p.m., Lesson Fourteen

Thank you for showing up even though you're not feeling your best today. You thought this might help with your cranky, contrary, self-pitying mood and it will. Keeping on with your obligations even when you don't feel up to it is helpful. It empowers you because you're doing something to take charge of feeling better rather than sinking further into helplessness, wrongly concluding you cannot control your moods. *[I was indeed so irritable that I could barely stand to be around myself—you know the feeling. Though I was vaguely aware that my cranky, self-pitying mood was self-sabotaging and way out of proportion to any real life events, I also knew myself well enough to realize my ill-tempered mood hid other emotions that I didn't understand. Honestly,*

I battled with myself between staying stuck in my icky mood so I wouldn't have to face what was underneath or finding my courage to face whatever I had stuffed. Courage won out only because I showed up to journal despite my foul mood . . . and, I believe, the detective part of myself wanted to know what was causing all the emotional ruckus.]

You're out of sorts in part due to the emotional work of closing your practice and helping patients manage their feelings and the effects on them. Your dream last night also had a carryover effect on today's mood. You dreamed of being sent to a war zone with a platoon of men and being given the first target assignment without any information or assistance in what to expect except that it involved danger. Your dream ended with your realization that you'd have to wait and see what happened and deal with whatever came up since your efforts to prepare were not working. *[Yes, real life bumps and stresses aren't exactly things we can plan and control; we sort out how best to manage them as they come up.]*

The dream was, indeed, another communication about the unsuitability of your efforts to approach your retirement in a planned, step-by-step linear way with an expected outcome. Ending relationships and your work with patients as a psychologist is ending your career. This is an unfolding process. It involves relationships and feelings which will manifest in their own ways. It's not something that can be predicted and controlled.

The dream also pointed out that your retirement, the first target assignment which was likely to be dangerous, is more emotionally stressful than you acknowledge. Also, the dream commander's nonchalant attitude in the face of your anxious attempts to get information to prepare for the dangerous assignment reflects the current attitude you try to present that your retirement is no big deal. The truth is somewhere in between. It's not dangerous and it's not insignificant. It's a process with feelings you'll face as you get closer to the target—the ending of your career work. *[I love the beautiful simplicity of this reminder that a balanced attitude, a middle road, is best in preparing for and adjusting to life transitions. Retirement involves major change and unknowns which usually elicit a mix of emotions. The changes and accompanying emotions are significant but not dangerous. They are important to acknowledge so I can say goodbye to the old and welcome whatever new experiences are ahead.]*

The dream also communicates that your attempts to seek direction on your retirement by using masculine linear problem-solving will not help. It's not possible to plan all the steps in such a life transition. Retirement involves endings, loss, mourning, fears, and anxieties. It also represents new beginnings, opportunities, change, and excitement. These simply have to be lived. They can't be planned or scheduled. It's important to stay present in adjusting to this transition. Do not allow discouragement or the feelings of upheaval and uncertainty that accompany change to take over. They are temporary, like everything. Simply observe and release them as they arise. No need to over-identify with any of the feelings associated with a change of this magnitude.

Preparing for this intellectually, which you've done masterfully, is different from the emotional experience. You know this but forgot or deny that it applies to you too. *[My inner teacher said this in a teasing, lighthearted way.]* You don't need a step-by-step manual to direct you through this process. Follow your heart's intuition and stop expecting so much from yourself. Just face the experience as it unfolds without fear. Trust your own and your patients' capacity for managing this in a way that is both affirming and meaningful.

Your cranky, irritable mood today actually reflects underlying sadness due to the normal loss you feel with ending your professional vocation and saying goodbye to patients you care about. That's enough for today. *[Such a simple explanation—crankiness was hiding sadness. Amazing the lengths some of us will go to in order to avoid the normal sadness of loss. My mood has shifted and is lighter after today's lesson. It's a relief to honestly feel the sadness and know its source. I'm also grateful to have the non-cranky version of myself back—that will also be much better for the others I'll be with today.]*

Personal Reflections

Today's lesson was akin to a therapy session with my inner teacher. I received helpful assistance in understanding my cranky mood, interpreting last night's dream, and clarifying unacknowledged feelings regarding my retirement at the end of this year.

Fascinating to learn this intuitive journaling can be effective in interpreting dreams related to current issues and events in my life. After seeing how helpful a tool it was for interpreting last night's dreams, I have since used it deliberately whenever I had dreams or other intuitive images I needed more help understanding. I simply write out the dream or image, using the same preparatory process outlined in the introduction.

I have kept a dream journal for many years and still do. I view dreams as helpful messages from our subconscious mind or the higher Self to facilitate personal growth and learning. Though I became proficient in interpreting most of my dream symbols and characters and relating dream messages to relevant life events, there were some dreams whose meaning I was never able to discern. With others, it might take days or weeks to clarify dream messages related to my life at that time. In working with dreams over the years, I came to see that there are often layers of meanings to dream symbols. With my traditional method of interpreting dreams, I was not always satisfied that I had correctly discerned the deeper layers of the dream message. The symbolic and metaphoric nature of dream symbols and images can make interpretation uncertain.

The discovery of intuitive writing as another tool for interpretation of these subconscious messages from the higher Self was exciting. I found the use of intuitive journaling to be a faster, more incisive way of interpreting dream images, symbols, and messages as they relate to my life. It seemed to quickly get to the layer of meaning I most needed.

Interestingly, my dream recall has lessened noticeably over the years I have used intuitive journaling. To me, this suggests that as I get more intuitive information to facilitate personal and spiritual growth through journaling, there is less need to convey this through dream recall.

Inner Guidance Is always Available

11/4/06, 7:00 a.m., Lesson Fifteen

The quietness of early morning is peaceful and inspiring. This is reflected in the moments you observe nature through your kitchen window. Just look at those mountains. Even the trees are silent and still as if joining you in this time of quiet communion with me.

Open your heart and mind. Listen to the thoughts I send. This silent interaction is communion in the stillness and quiet within. Most of the time, you're so busy rushing around and thinking of all the things you have to do or just letting your mind and thoughts drift that this kind of communication—communion—is barely possible. *[This is so true. Living in the future with my mind in runaway mode distracts me from being present and living from the stillness within. Today's experience of communication as communion reveals what is possible when I am fully present with each moment from this inner stillness. This communion as communication is a powerful way of approaching daily life and all interactions.]*

As you are beginning to know through direct experience, it is necessary to quiet distractions and outward focus in order to connect with the stillness within. That is why all forms of meditation teach ways to quiet mental chatter and other distractions. *[Though I've had a regular meditation practice since 1992, I still get lots of practice with noticing the multitude of ways my mind wanders. From what I've read and experienced personally, it is the nature of the mind and ego to be caught up in distractions. Expecting and accepting this are helpful in noticing, then releasing the distractions without fighting them.]*

For many years, you did not know how or even believe it was possible to have this kind of direct access and communication with the world of spirit through your higher Self. So we used other ways of communicating—dreams, intuition, the timely arrival of certain books, people, or experiences into your life. We have been working behind the scenes even during the times you were unaware of our presence and guidance. *[This is a good example of the limiting effects of our beliefs. At some level, I did not believe it was possible to communicate with my higher Self and the interpenetrating spirit plane of consciousness while in physical life. How inspiring and comforting to know that spirit never withdrew nor broke contact just because I was oblivious, unaware, or didn't take the time to discover the stillness within where I could connect with my higher Self and the world of spirit. Spirit, including my higher Self, never gave up and simply accepted and worked with me where I was.]*

This direct access is possible because of your growth and openness to the potential for more over the past many years. Ongoing and persistent work led to new opportunities for learning and growth. You are getting used to this more direct communication during our work sessions. *[Each time I repeat the intuitive journaling is like rediscovering the connection with my higher Self and spirit all over again, as if I haven't quite assimilated it yet. So it's a delightful experience each time to be reminded of the connection and communication with my higher Self and spirit. Looking back, I can see that my persistent willingness and openness to using this guidance even when I was less aware eventually led to more conscious awareness of and direct access to the constant presence of inner guidance.]*

Your recent intuitive understanding—your "aha" experience as you would call it—that this is available and accessible anytime as long as you focus inward and request it was part of your adjustment to integrating this experience of direct communication with spirit. *[This was like a deeper emotional understanding of what was happening. Previously, I understood it intellectually, but with this intuitive experience I understood the enormity of what was happening at an emotional level. A truly humbling experience.]*

Learning to stay open to this guidance and intuitive communication at all times even when you're doing other things is unfamiliar to you and will continue to take practice. It's possible to function in your daily physical world and body and still have your inner observer turned on, so to speak. You'll be able to listen for inner guidance at any time. It takes awareness, intention, and choice. The practice of this allows you to integrate the presence and benefits of inner stillness and its connection with the world of spirit.

So, do you see how this fits together? First comes the awareness that you are more than a physical body; you are, in fact, spirit in physical form. *[I understood this intellectually earlier in my life when I was studying Edgar Cayce and other metaphysical writers. I began to grasp this at a deeper, emotional level through direct experiences during meditation. Still, comprehending and applying this concept of being spirit in physical form in day-to-day life is, like most things, an ongoing process of remembering and integrating.]*

Then comes accessing and developing your connection with your soul through all the ways available for spiritual development, one of the best of which is meditation. *[This has been true for me because of the direct experience or glimpses of deep peace, stillness, love, and connection with something greater during meditation. Though I recall similar experiences using guided imagery and visualization, being outside in nature, prayer, and being around babies or children, it is meditation that has been the best way for me to deepen this experienced connection with something greater. Finding the ways of connecting with your own higher Self that work for you and being consistent in using them seems to be the key. A regular meditation practice is not easy but the benefits are enormous.]*

Then comes the practice of accessing inner stillness through meditation and seeing the benefits. *[When I first started a regular meditation practice, I saw mostly resistance for six weeks in the form of physical discomfort, monkey mind, and every imaginable distraction and excuse not to practice. I only had glimmers of inner stillness and the benefits of quiet mind-body-spirit in the beginning. The classes I had taken helped prepare me for what to expect and how to respond to distractions. Even so, I was appalled at the level of resistance I encountered. Without the classes from teachers well trained in meditation and my commitment to persist, I would likely have given up on myself as a failure in quieting my mind. It's only when I accepted that it is the nature of the mind to be all over the place that I could shift my attitude from being appalled at the state of my mind's disarray to witnessing or observing the mind's antics without judgment, then redirecting it to the chosen focus for meditation. I am calmer, happier, more grounded, and clearer in my thinking as a result of meditation. I think it has also aided me in being more forgiving and accepting of myself and others. It clearly helped me face and understand my fears more deeply.]*

Then comes the awareness that you can communicate with your higher Self and teachers in spirit through a variety of means that all require openness and asking. *[Prior to intuitive journaling, I experienced such communication through dreams, meditation, and sometimes intuitively in crisis situations.]*

Then comes the awareness that this does not occur only during meditation or times of writing such as this but

81

has the potential to be co-occurring with your physical life experiences if your intention and desire to do so allow you to remain connected to your inner stillness as much as possible. *[Honestly, this remains difficult for me. I'm definitely at the beginning stages of a work in progress.]*

Then comes ongoing use and practice of these awarenesses in the never-ending cycle of learning, growing, and furthering your spiritual development which is then reflected in your physical body and life.

That's the end of today's teaching.

Personal Reflections

I'm still surprised by the number of opportunities that slip by me in terms of applying things I think I've learned. That too is a process, I've discovered. So, I am inconsistent in applying what I'm learning. Sometimes, as with my efforting, it's even hard to remember the lesson or notice when I've reverted to thinking I can control outcomes with my effort. As a result, the same lesson is repeated in a multitude of ways as if to assure me that I'll get it if I keep on listening and practicing, doing my best.

Looking back over a period of years, I see signs of gradual integration of what I'm learning. As I assimilate one lesson, a new or revised form of that lesson is given that keeps me moving slowly forward in my learning about how to live from my higher Self. Most of the time my energy level, health, relationships with others, and happiness with myself and life are better, though this also has its ups and downs. I still get grumpy, fatigued, discouraged, scared, and worried. But I notice and address these energy depleting reactions more quickly.

When I notice I've gotten off track, I am quicker to take responsibility for understanding and correcting my part in what needs to be changed. The times I don't notice when I'm off track are times my energy flags, I get sick, am moody, and difficult to be around. These are usually my cues that there's something important I'm ignoring. I can choose to stay stuck in my self-defeating negativity or not. My goal is to notice and listen to these signs sooner rather than later, and to do the best I can assimilating the lessons I'm offered.

LESSON SIXTEEN

Savoring the Experience of Nature's Beauty

11/09/06, 5:50 p.m. from Mazatlan, Mexico, Lesson Sixteen

I am here with you. The sunset is majestic, lighting the sky in shades of orange over the ocean and Deer Island. The water is soothing as it rolls in waves to lap the shore. Aaahh— such beauty and calm reflected in nature's ocean and the setting of the sun over the water. *[As I reread this 6 years later, I can still hear the waves, sense and feel the expansive peacefulness and breathtaking awe of this glorious fading of sun's light. It is nature's grand finale uniquely designed for each day's end. This sensation of watching the sun's setting is akin to the fading from one state of consciousness to another as we move from wakefulness to sleep or even, I imagine, the transition from physical life to life in spirit.]*

Personal Reflections

The shortness of this lesson left me doubting its validity. I realized my teacher was reminding me that lessons need not be long to be meaningful. Sometimes short is good. Simply rereading this brief lesson allows me to re-experience with the inner senses the spacious beauty and peace of the sunset and the ocean's waves.

In reviewing some of the previous lessons in my journal, I was struck by the similarity between the current lessons and those written in the intuitive journaling format adapted from Julia Cameron beginning with the starter phrase, If my soul spoke to me now. Both formats access similar inner wisdom and knowledge. I initially thought that Cameron's simpler exercise was different from the intuitive process I became accustomed to using for these lessons. This limited perception interfered with my seeing that the two formats are simply different ways of tapping the same source of inner wisdom. My belief that there is a certain perfect or right way to do things once again created this interference.

Now I understand why my teacher repeats things for me—like her patient reminders that I make preparation more difficult than it need be. I see now that I can accomplish the same thing by beginning my intuitive journaling with the simple phrase, If my soul spoke to me now, as I can by listening for her inner voice after centering, writing out my intention, and reciting a prayer of protection. The point is that there is no right or perfect way to do this, just different ways that suit different people. I simply prefer the one I use most often, though both approaches yield the same results and access the same source within.

The repetition of much of the information in the lessons in different ways reflects my teacher's patience and nonjudgment. It mirrors a reality of life in that repetition of information in a variety of ways is often necessary to help us fully absorb and apply it.

It's wonderful to see that learning, growth, and change are always possible; it's never too late. I'm grateful and relieved to know my inner teacher never wearies or gives up because I need so much repetition to assimilate my lessons. It also gives me great hope that perhaps I can aspire to such an attitude of patient acceptance and nonjudgment with others as they work to integrate their own lessons in ways best suited to them. *[As you can see, like my teacher, I repeat and repeat too!]*

LESSON SEVENTEEN

Drops in the Ocean of Love

11/12/06, 10 a.m., from Mexico, Lesson Seventeen

[Based on the last lesson, I began today's session with the starter phrase, If my soul spoke to me now. The first half of the beginning text sentence reflects that. As before, the italic print represents my words; the regular print is my teacher's voice.]

If my soul spoke to me now it would remind me to be lighter of heart. Do not let yourself be brought down by negative feelings.

Think of the clearness of the water off Deer Island, how refreshing it was. Think of the lightness that washes over you when you are a part of nature. Later you can use the memory of that feeling and experience to bring about the same feeling. Use of imagery in this way, as you already know, is a tool to disrupt a negative mood and replace it

87

with one that is positive and uplifting. Recall the positive memory and the associated feeling, then feel that positive emotion in your heart center. Yes, you're doing it now and it feels lighter, more positive. *[This is another good example of this interactive mental communication. She immediately acknowledged my practicing what she was describing and the results it created.]*

You are a drop in the ocean of infinite love and peace. Forgetting this leaves you heavy with a sense of being separate and adrift. See your Self as part of and one with the Infinite. This is what brings you lightness and meaning.

Personal Reflections

Today's lesson was another reminder of the many ways imagery can be used to reduce the stressful effects of negativity by shifting to positive memories. Use of grateful feelings from the heart center has such power. It can reconnect me with lightness and peace.

Gratitude creates an expansive, energized, and uplifted feeling. It's as if my heart reaches out to encompass all of nature and humanity at such moments. This is what Christel Nani, author of the CD "Transforming Your Archetypes," would call choosing a high vibration response. Negativity and helplessness create a depleting low vibration response. Despite the obvious powerful, positive effects of heartfelt gratitude, it is far too easy to revert to habitual negative thoughts. The lesson is to notice whether I'm creating a high or low vibration response in my choice of thoughts and feelings in a given situation, then changing my response if it's called for.

The heart-opening metaphor my inner teacher used— you are a drop in the ocean of infinite love and peace—was a powerful reminder of each of us being part of and one with the Infinite. Simply repeating this beautiful phrase evokes a feeling of oneness and deep tranquility. It will be a good visualization and affirmation to use on a regular basis. Hopefully, it will disrupt my tendency to revert to that low vibration response of feeling separate and alone.

Since each of our souls is a drop in the ocean of infinite love, we are all connected in being a part of and one with the Infinite. What an exhilarating, uniting awareness.

LESSON
EIGHTEEN

Growth Requires Practice and Patience

11/15/06, 7:30 a.m., Lesson Eighteen

The information your friend sent you about an energy health conference taught by a Chinese holistic physician sparks your interest. It's because you know the value of meditation, qigong, and yoga from your own experience. Yet the required practice of these arts in the 90 days prior to attending puts you off. *[Yes, I'm wondering how I'll fit this in.]* It's purely to prepare yourself for the additional learning and healing you'll get at the conference.

This is another layer of learning about self, relationships, and the world, all of which can be improved through intentional use of energy and strengthening of the body's energy centers. Begin the preparations as if you were going to attend the conference. You've set goals to expand your meditation and yoga practice and resume practice of qigong but not yet implemented them. This is a fine time to begin.

[Though I did not attend the conference, this lesson helped encourage me to be more creatively flexible about ways to free up time for things of importance to me. I expanded time for yoga, meditation, family/friends, and writing with elimination of most evening TV time and discovered I was much happier and less stressed.]

Your thought today about continuing the twenty to thirty minute daily yoga routine you had on vacation was a great idea. You're wondering where you'll find time for all of this. Although morning is a good time to practice yoga, it's beneficial anytime and will have relaxation benefits if used at nighttime. You have noticed we have been introducing small changes to help you learn to be more flexible. Soon you'll be finding other ways of tending to responsibilities while also maintaining regular practice of meditation, intuitive writing, yoga, and qigong. There is time for it all!

Walking is a good exercise alternative because it gets you outside in nature. Just be flexible about when and how long you do these health enhancing activities. Give up the notion that you're too tired or undisciplined to do these activities at nighttime; it's just not true. You have plenty of energy and discipline but it's simply not a strong habit or conditioned response to use your evening time this way . . . yet. Your distorted belief that you're too tired to get yourself to do this on your own in the evening has gotten in the way of doing it. Change! Reverse gears! Just start to practice in the evening whether or not you're tired. Notice your response. Does it calm, relax, re-energize, recharge you? *[I know it does. I also feel more empowered when I move forward instead of staying stuck and making excuses for it.]*

This training and discipline are needed to prepare for learning and work still ahead. So be patient with yourself. Practice being flexible. Integrate these exercises that feed your spiritual growth, renew your body, and develop your mind.

That's enough for today.

Personal Reflections

Integrating my teacher's excellent suggestions into daily life seemed overwhelming at first. I didn't know where I'd find the time to add the worthwhile activities. The clarity with which my inner teacher presented the reasons for my difficulty implementing these changes helped encourage me to look for more creative solutions.

I realized I could integrate more of these healthy activities by reducing TV time. This was easier than I expected as I discovered I felt more energized, relaxed, and calm with the expanded activities and less TV exposure. It required the most discipline to break the established TV habit, although it had never really recharged my energy as I pretended it did.

Looking back from the perspective of more limited and selective media exposure, I see more clearly the level of stress I was unwittingly creating with my past nighttime mental diet of TV entertainment. This was a helpful reminder that what I choose to feed my mind is as important in regulating my overall health and wellbeing as what I feed my body.

LESSON NINETEEN

Time to Say Goodbye

11/19/06, 7:30 a.m., Lesson Nineteen

The walk this morning was helpful and refreshing, was it not? The emotional heaviness you have been feeling is related to the anticipated intensity of your final five weeks of helping your patients through this transition. You feel the pain they experience in adjusting to this unsought, stressful change brought about by your retirement.

At the same time, you're excited and ready for this new phase of your life's learning. Yes, it's a bit like dying and being ready to move on into the world of spirit; you want to go but feel the sadness, fear, pain, and difficulty letting go of those left behind. It's alright. A mix of feelings is perfectly natural, even experiencing them all at the same time. They are all important learning experiences and times of great potential growth for you and your patients. It's up to each of you whether you view and use these times of change as opportunities for growth and learning. You can find a way to remind them, as well as yourself, of this.

Partings have been difficult for you. They are for most people. You've had many opportunities to work on this with the deaths of your parents, grandparents, numerous relatives, and friends. Try to remember, from the perspective of spirit, that all souls live on after physical death; they continue to serve, learn, and grow.

These goodbyes to patients with whom you've worked in therapy and learned much from are another lesson in the impermanence of all things. The growth you've made personally has enriched your professional work with others and will never be lost. Likewise, the growth others have made enriches their lives as well as yours.

I am always here for you in spirit as are your loved ones who have passed into spirit before you. We are all interested in your continued growth and learning and are here to support and assist you however we can. There are no limits except your desire and request for our assistance. You are beginning to be more aware of the constant presence of those helpers in spirit who love and care for you and choose to express their love by helping when asked. *[Knowing helpers in spirit are always available to assist is both comforting and inspiring. From later intuitive journaling, I understood that our asking for help is necessary to avoid our own free will being interfered with by spirit. Though I have had numerous intuitive experiences involving deceased loved ones, my inner teacher is distinctly different from any of them. My intuitive experiences with deceased loved ones have occurred in the context of intuitive journaling, meditative states, or dreams. Some were to prepare me for the passing of loved ones. Others were clearly to encourage my own spiritual development and to allow for forgiveness and resolution of unfinished lessons. All these experiences provided reassurance that loved ones live on and continue to learn and grow in spirit.]*

We know you are worried about your office building being under contract for sale. You're worried that if the sale goes through in mid-December, as planned, you will need to find new space and move to another location at the most stressful period of closing your psychology practice. Let go of your worry. Trust the process. Trust that whatever happens is exactly what's needed and serves a purpose in the bigger picture. Regardless of what happens, we're here to help and guide your decisions and management of this. View this as an unfolding opportunity for all and choose to be curious rather than worried. We know that particular reframe is a new one, even to you. Give it a try. *[My teacher said this with affectionate, teasing humor. I laughed aloud at the delightful, lighthearted reframing of worry to "choose to be curious." She is using some of the same skills for reframing negative thoughts that I teach patients, reminding me to practice what I teach.]*

That's enough for today.

Personal Reflections

As I prepare to close my thirty years of clinical practice as a psychologist and retire, I recognize this has been an emotionally intense time. In assisting patients with managing this change, facilitating their transition to new therapists, and finding meaningful ways to say goodbye, I have come to admire the remarkable resilience of humans.

My stress levels were intensified during this time when the building that housed our leased office space was placed on the market. It was uncertain whether we would need to move to new office space even as I was closing my practice. The smiling humor in today's lesson about reframing my worry to an attitude of curiosity—don't worry, be curious—was the perfect touch of lightness. This simple act of detaching from worry to observe with curiosity the unfolding of events, confident of managing whatever came about, was both powerful and empowering.

Being reminded that assistance is always available for the asking was clearly needed as I had cut myself off from this awareness with my worried preoccupation. The contrast between my own and my inner teacher's responses to the possibility of having to move to new office space during this stressful transition was striking. The low energy I created with my worry was in stark contrast to my teacher's buoyant, confident, hopeful energy and a reminder of all the support I have from spirit. All I had to do was ask. So I did. I set a gratitude intention for all the necessary help and assistance in finding the best affordable office space.

As it turned out, our building sold though we had more time than expected. However, rent increased beyond what we could afford. Since my business partner (also my husband) planned to continue practicing after I retired, moving was necessary. I found a better, affordable office space within a few miles of our old office; we moved the early part of the following year. Using the reminders in this lesson helped immensely with keeping this entire process more positive.

LESSON TWENTY

The Power of Mental Visualization

11/20/06 7:30 a.m., Lesson Twenty

I know your energy is low and you're still not feeling up to par because of your cold. Let me help recharge your energy through this exercise: feel my hands on your brow and heart. *[Although this is done mentally through thoughts, I can feel the sensation of my inner teacher's hands on my forehead and heart.]*

This is a tool for sending healing light to you where it's most needed. Don't be afraid to visualize taking in as much of this healing light energy as you need. There's an endless supply. The more you use, the more there is to draw upon for both of us. *[I stop writing as I do this mental visualization exercise for several minutes. I soak up the relaxed feelings as the tension releases from my facial muscles. After a few minutes of this, I am able to breathe more easily and my congestion lessens.]*

See how it works? It's similar to the transformative breathing exercise you teach patients. In this exercise, breathe in the light of harmony and balance to the troubled places in your body and breathe out stuck, stale energy. Your vision is crisper now; your head is less congested. *[I'm surprised at the level of relief this provided after only a few minutes.]*

Yes, in response to your mental question, combining Thought Field Therapy and this breath would also be helpful in boosting your energy and reducing your cold symptoms. *[Thought Field Therapy is the trademark name of an energy treatment tool developed by psychologist Roger Callahan, Ph.D. It is based on the same principles as acupuncture but uses tapping on body treatment points associated with the meridian system to restore balance to the energy system. If done correctly, this rapidly helps clear symptoms that are the focus of treatment. Gary Craig developed a version of this approach called Emotional Freedom Techniques (EFT) which is available online for readers interested in learning more about this energy balancing tool.]*

The universe is composed of energy. This approach of visualizing healing light, releasing blocked energy with the outbreath, and breathing in perfectly balanced healing light energy can be used for anything. As long as you do not get attached to having a certain outcome, you acknowledge there is a bigger picture you do not know or control, and you learn from the problem, this approach is always beneficial in bringing about positive change.

The change may not appear in the form you expect or in the way you wish. It will be what you need at that time.

Yes, in response to your mental question, even using this visualization approach for your friends who need to sell their home is beneficial, particularly because they asked for help with this. *[Details below.]*

Your use of mental visualization in this way implies a level of belief in the underlying energy which governs all things. Although this Source is beyond us, the guiding force of this Infinite Intelligence in combination with our efforts and intentions makes things work. Just think—in combination with us! Use this energy of light that is in and around all things; it is a creation of Source. There is no darkness or problem that the light cannot penetrate and heal.

The form the healing takes or the result may be other than what you want or expect, so stay open to what happens. Trust this process to provide exactly what is needed for you at that time. It offers the potential for learning, growth, and service, although that is up to you. You can resist what is, rail against it, or accept the reality of what is and look for ways to gratefully acknowledge the lessons it offers of love, acceptance, forgiveness, patience, and self-responsibility. It offers a new way of viewing yourself and the world.

That's enough for today.

Personal Reflections

After practicing the mental visualization exercises my teacher suggested for my cold and low energy, I did indeed feel less congested, less fatigued, and my vision was crisper. Though I knew basic self-care of more rest, fluids, and keeping stress managed were still necessary to assist my body with healing, it was a refreshing reminder of the power of positive visualization to relieve symptoms and suffering while assisting the body's natural efforts toward restoring balance and health. Since I have seen beneficial results from use of visualization exercises both with patients and in my own personal life, I was pleased to get new ideas for its use.

Everyone visualizes—if you notice the delicious smell of pastries or baking bread, you're visualizing through smell. When you notice worried or resentful thoughts, happy memories or pleasant thoughts of a recent accomplishment, you are visualizing through thoughts. When you can see in your mind's eye an endearing smile or behavior of a loved one, you are visualizing through mental pictures. My sensing my inner teacher's invisible hands on my forehead and heart was another example of visualizing through sensation. Unfortunately, many people have the mistaken idea that they cannot visualize because mental pictures do not come easily for them. In fact, visualization includes thoughts, feelings, sensations, smells as well as mental pictures or any combination of these.

One of the most common forms of negative visualization is everyday worry. If you practice noticing your thoughts, you'll begin to pay attention to the feeling quality of your thoughts. Most of us can see the tension, strain, and misery we create for ourselves with our running inner dialogue of worry, criticism, or irritation. So it's not surprising that positive use of visualization can be equally powerful with substantial stress-reducing results. To work effectively, our level of belief in the positive visualization must be consistent at all levels of our awareness, including the unconscious level. The same is true for positive affirmations.

In talking about the value of visualization with friends who needed to sell their home before they could afford to relocate, we all agreed to visualize the best successful sale outcome for them. I learned two months later that their home sold within six weeks of initiating this joint, planned visualization. It's a much better use of mental energy than worrying! Thoughts are energy too; what we consistently focus on we energize, empower, and draw to ourselves.

As with lesson four, at the time of today's intuitive lesson I was unaware of Reiki, a form of healing touch, and its similarity with my inner teacher's first exercise to help recharge my energy. After completing Reiki training years later, I recognized the simultaneous touching of my forehead and heart while sending healing light energy where it was needed was, indeed, like Reiki which means universal life force energy.

I had no knowledge of Reiki prior to 2009. Yet, life circumstances brought me in touch [no pun intended!] with a friend who was learning Reiki and needed to practice on someone. The experience of receiving Reiki was deeply relaxing yet energizing. Since Reiki is, in my view, another way of restoring balance to the subtle energy system, it appealed to me. To this day, I continue to benefit from its use with myself and others nearly every day. Is it possible that my higher Self and inner teacher, bound by neither time nor space, knew of my future pursuit of Reiki and chose to include samples of Reiki healing touch for that reason?

Adopt a Daily Attitude of Gratitude

11/23/06, 7:30 a.m., Thanksgiving Day, Lesson Twenty-One

Every day is cause for thanks giving. Exercising gratitude and thankfulness on a daily basis is uplifting to the body, mind, and soul. It creates the mental attitude from which to approach each day. Paying attention to what you're grateful for throughout each day creates a relaxed, positive frame of mind. This, in turn, creates clarity in problem-solving. An attitude of gratefulness for what you have counters the stress in your lives; it reduces tension and negativity. You're more open.

It's hard to consistently remember to practice gratitude. It's especially difficult when faced with challenges like illness; lack of money; lack of resources to meet basic needs; fear; anger; jealousy; loss of work, health, or loved ones.

However, if you are courageous enough to practice gratitude even at those times, it fosters physical, mental, and emotional health and connects you with spirit, with something larger than yourself. It's easy to give in to fear, resentment, anger, self-pity, discouragement, pessimism, and loss of hope when faced with challenges that seem overwhelming and create struggle in your lives. Life is the hardest when basic survival needs are not being met or are threatened in some way. Trusting you will be cared for and provided for at such times when you make your best effort and get nowhere seems impossible; it's hard to even come up with things for which to be grateful. That's not to say there is nothing to be grateful for at those times. You are just unable to see them.

The perception and creation of peace and gratitude begin within each of you. If just one person experiences heartfelt gratitude and peace, it affects everyone whether or not you are aware of it. The presence of a baby often creates an opening of your hearts to love, peace, and smiles. Regardless of your current circumstances, you can use the mind's imagination to visualize or remember times that create an opening of the heart and feelings of hope, gratitude, love, or upliftment.

Be your inner light today and let gratitude, peace, and love infuse everything. *[This larger perspective of allowing heartfelt gratitude to permeate everything is an ideal to which I aspire. When applying this to daily life, I notice how easily I get off center and lose my connection with my inner light. This is especially true during times of increased or prolonged stress. I know this is happening whenever I'm stuck in negativity. At those times, I realize my heart has closed and my inner light and energy have dimmed. If I pay attention to the multitude of benevolent signs of something greater all around me, there are lots of helpful things I can choose to reopen my heart and turn my gratitude light back on: spontaneous thoughts that remind me to breathe deeply, slow down, stretch, or walk outdoors; thoughtful gestures; smiles; the playful antics of animals or children; nature's aromas, sounds, and sights; music; singing, writing, or drawing; prayer; meditation. The times I'm able to use these reminders to realign with my inner light and its heartfelt gratitude, my hope and joy are restored. My energy level improves too.]*

Personal Reflections

It's hard to even imagine how different things would be in our lives and the world if we all focused on feelings of gratitude and appreciation throughout the day. I have no doubt that this, in itself, would facilitate a transformation in consciousness.

The Institute of HeartMath's research presented by Childre and Martin in *The HeartMath Solution* provides objective data regarding the highly positive physical, mental, and emotional effects of maintaining an attitude of gratitude from the heart center. Their research shows that our emotional states are reflected in our heart's rhythmic patterns. Since all the body systems, including the nervous system, entrain to the heart's rhythm, our emotions have powerful effects far beyond what most of us realize. Positive, heart-based feelings like compassion, care, nonjudgment, sincere appreciation, and forgiveness create a smooth, coherent heart rhythm pattern. The resulting, cascading effects of coherence throughout our entire system allow it to function in a balanced, harmonious, energy efficient manner. Some of the benefits of this physiological coherence include improved hormonal balance (e.g., level of stress hormone, cortisol); enhanced immune response; a calm nervous system; lower blood pressure; increased efficiency of the brain's information processing functions needed for thinking clearly, problem-solving, and effective decision-making; a general sense of well-being; optimization of our regenerative level of energy which allows for more efficient, productive use of energy. On the other hand, negative feelings such as worry, anxiety, anger, judgment, or guilt create irregular, incoherent heart rhythm and physiological response patterns. The effects of this system-wide pattern of incoherence include hormonal imbalances (e.g., increased cortisol); suppressed immune response; higher blood pressure; difficulty relaxing, concentrating, and thinking clearly; reduced efficiency of higher level brain functions resulting in a narrower perspective in viewing difficult situations and identifying effective solutions; feeling drained; and depleted energy. This research makes it abundantly clear that evoking sincere, heart-based, positive feelings in a consistent, deliberate way has a powerful restorative, nourishing, and balancing impact on the entire body system at every level.

This lesson inspired me to journal about all the things I was grateful for today. What an uplifting, spacious feeling that created! More often, I simply do that in my thoughts. Imperfect as I am, I can still choose, as often I am able, to find the beauty, joy, gratitude, and love that are present each moment. Direct expression of genuine appreciation and care in my daily interactions with others is a reward in itself. It creates positive energy from the heart wherever I go. It acknowledges others' contributions and uplifts both the giver and receiver. The positive effects persist and carry over, encouraging us to pass this uplifting energy along to others.

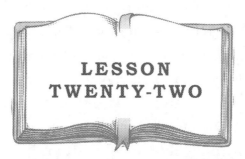

LESSON TWENTY-TWO

The World of Spirit

11/27/06, 7:30 a.m., Lesson Twenty-Two

I am here beside you admiring the gorgeous scene from your dining room: Pikes Peak dusted with snow, towering in the distance as it reaches toward the cloudless blue sky. The magnificence of nature touches our souls and uplifts us. This feeling of joy and peace are constants in the hereafter, in the world of spirit.

Imagine a dimension where there is no time—no rush, pressure, or deadlines. That is the world of spirit.

Imagine a place of unforgettable beauty, color, and sounds where love, joy, and peace are ever present. A place of eternal learning with mentors, teachers, and helpers for all that is needed to assist in each soul's growth. This is the world of spirit.

Imagine a place without the constraints of time or space where you can communicate instantly through thoughts and create things loved or fondly remembered from your physical life on earth through thought. This is the world of spirit.

Imagine a place with no judgment, only unconditional love and acceptance. This is the world of spirit.

Imagine a place where we can see and experience every thought, feeling, behavior, and action we had during our physical life on earth and the effect they had on others. In this way, we examine the growth and work, or lack thereof, toward our life's purpose while we were in the school of physical life on earth. This is the world of spirit—a place of ongoing learning and preparation for advancement to more enlightened levels if we choose.

It is a place of freedom to exercise our will in service to others and work toward our own return to the Universal Divine Light. Imagine a place where we grasp the bigger purpose and how all the events and happenings in our physical lives and world fit together to serve a greater plan of returning each of us to our Source and manifesting spirit in the physical. This is the world of spirit.

Experiences in physical life that touch our souls, that open and lift our hearts and spirit, are reminders of the world of spirit.

Personal Reflections

This lesson's description of the world of spirit stands in stark contrast to the physical world in which we live.

Yet, as my inner teacher said in prior lessons, the spiritual and physical worlds are part of the same oneness that permeates all of life. As spiritual beings in physical bodies, how do we go about expressing our true spiritual nature, however imperfectly, while living in the physical world? How do we create the qualities of spirit in our physical lives on earth—a world of peace, joy, beauty, unconditional love, nonjudgment, free will, and self-responsibility for our growth?

It seems to me this is an inner journey we each have to make. One of freely choosing to awaken to our spiritual nature, to connect with the soul's inner stillness and wisdom, and to willingly participate in our soul's growth in order to return to our natural state of oneness with Source. It involves honest self-examination, commitment to growth, and responsibility for searching within for meaningful answers to the universal questions: Who am I? Why am I here? What is my purpose?

Though this is an imperfect process for all of us, prior lessons have consistently pointed to inner change as the starting point. Since qualities of spirit such as peace, unconditional love, joy, nonjudgment, nonattachment, and compassion begin within each of us and move outward to impact the whole, it seems to me that doing our best to live from the inner wisdom of our higher Self through an open heart-mind is a worthy guiding principle in this process. If in doubt about whether our thoughts, speech, and deeds reflect the positive, high vibration energy of our higher Self, we can tune in to its inner wisdom and guidance.

Those of you who have experienced moments of open-hearted expansion—where you feel at one with something greater that is a loving presence beyond any human description—know these are unforgettable. During intuitive journaling on 1/26/2011, I asked what I needed to do to live within this unconditional love that permeates everything. The response was that I needed "to raise my vibrations and keep them high." I asked, what raises my vibrations? Love, in all its manifestations, I was told. Examples of manifestations of love given by my inner teacher included living from the heart; grateful, appreciative behavior; going with the flow of life; heart-opening experiences such as stirring music, a baby's smile, and nature's unpretentious grandeur; joy; meaningful sharing with others in need and those open to learning and growth; and seeing beyond the facade of every individual to their core of divine light.

The things I find most noticeably helpful in raising and keeping my vibrations high are practicing open-hearted gratitude and appreciation; keeping a hope-filled, optimistic attitude; committing time for spiritual development with meditation, intuitive journaling, affirmations, and being in nature; forgiving, making amends for harm I cause; treating others the way I wish to be treated; sharing knowledge and skills to help others when asked; maintaining regular exercise, healthy sleep and eating habits; fostering strong, loving, and fun connections with family and friends; and encouraging my own and other's learning and growth.

The point, for me, is to do my best to simultaneously lead my inner spiritual and outer physical lives in an open-hearted way that reflect my higher Self. Though this is always a work in progress, any effort toward this goal has helped me understand there is a bigger picture to the significance of life's lessons. It also reminds me that the worlds of spirit and physical are not separate. They are both manifestations of the Oneness of all life.

LESSON TWENTY-THREE

Endings and Beginnings

11/28/06, 7:30 a.m., Lesson Twenty-Three

Let the wind *[it's very windy today]* move through you and clear away any debris, releasing all that is anxious and negative, leaving you clear and calm.

What would be a fitting ending to closing your psychology practice, you wonder? You're already in the process of doing it with the handwritten cards and small gifts you're giving your patients. This is meaningful to them and you. Also, your care and assistance in transferring their ongoing treatment to a new psychologist allows them the option to continue their work. The funny goodbye card from several patients is a reminder that a sense of lightness and humor helps to manage this change.

The increased wind energy today is a metaphor for the cleansing process you're going through in closing your psychology practice. Clearing out the debris from the past makes way for new energy and learning. If you remain attached to the past and fear letting it go, there is no room for new ideas and there will be no moving on with your life in a different way. So, clear away. Let a mighty wind come up that is fearless in its cleaning out debris and clutter! Keep what is useful for this new phase of your life and recycle the rest. Yes, in response to your mental question just now, all those articles and resource files you've saved can be let go. Support the local shredding economy! Shred old business records and tests that cannot be used or donated. This will be very freeing. Recycle your books to colleagues. *[I really enjoyed recycling my professional journals to the local college and testing equipment and books to colleagues who would continue to use them.]*

In response to your awareness of how difficult this is for you, it helps that you can smile in acknowledging your tendency to hold onto things, creating clutter in your life. It also helps that you can smile at my attempts at humoring you to clear out what will no longer be useful. This is another way of creating a fitting ending of your work as a practicing psychologist and saying goodbye to the career phase of your life. That means letting go of any attachment you have to defining yourself by your work or career and opening your heart-mind to other ways to serve, learn, and grow.

Goodbyes, after all, are an ending of something in that moment of time which opens the door to a new beginning in the next moment. *[What a wonderful reminder that each moment is a new opportunity, a mini ending and beginning.]*

Endings and beginnings are the natural flow of life as is change. This constant cycle of endings and beginnings offers opportunities to practice nonattachment; to be in and with the present moment to learn and grow; and to be one with the river of life, trusting that its flow will take you exactly where you need to be.

Go with the flow of the moment today. Be present to each moment.

Personal Reflections

Today's lesson contained a number of helpful hints for handling the many details of closing my clinical psychology practice. I welcomed the ideas for letting go of what I would no longer use. For example, donating and recycling books and other professional material to colleagues. I also appreciated the affirmation of the meaningful ways chosen to say goodbye and end work with long-term patients who will continue treatment with new therapists.

My inner teacher's humor in encouraging letting go of stuff no longer needed by recycling and donating helped lighten this process of ending my career phase. The funny card from several patients was also a delightful reminder of how useful humor is in managing difficult transitions. This fold-out card with an array of animals in every emotional state contained funny quips such as You're leaving? You'll do anything for attention, won't you? Was it something I said? Never forget the answer to any crisis: doughnuts!

I can choose my response to the ending of my career. I can focus on mourning what is being left behind; I can be fearful of the unknown. Or I can celebrate the excitement of changes and new learning ahead. Like most things, it is a mix of all. Looking back, I see that I have learned as much from my patients as they have from me.

I still have a long ways to go in moving with the flow of life and being present to each moment. The deep sense of harmony and contentment that accompany those moments of being fully present are powerfully rewarding. One of the ways my inner teacher encourages my being present is by drawing attention to the beauty of nature and the positive lessons it offers at that moment. In today's weather metaphor, for example, she used the strong winds as a symbol for cleansing and clearing out all that is negative and in the past so new energy can emerge.

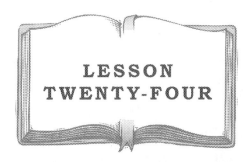

LESSON TWENTY-FOUR

Look for Beauty in all Things

11/30/06, 7:30 a.m., Lesson Twenty-Four

Everything is covered with pure white snow, and the sun is shining in a cloudless blue sky—nature's gift of a mantle over the earth that provides moisture for plants, the beauty of winter's landscape, and snow to play in.

The stillness that comes with the snowy landscape is a gift. Look for the beauty in all things, it says.

Winter weather and the difficulties it creates in getting out and about are helpful in drawing attention to your rush. A big snowstorm is a gift to enjoy. You can be quiet, stay indoors to cozy up with a book or indoor games, bake cookies, build a bookshelf, or take a nap.

Or you can go out and play in the snow with your kids, neighbors, or friends—skiing, sledding, making the first footprints in the fresh snowfall as you walk to the neighbors for hot chocolate.

The snow-covering of nature is like an infinite painting that produces calm and quiet within the heart. The snow crystals sparkle as the sun finds the snow, causing a brightness that makes you close your eyes to soak up its peace and light. Savor the beauty of nature blanketed in snow. The heartfelt gratitude and awe it inspires fills the day with the lightness of a snowflake. *[This experience of feeling nature's beauty warms and opens my heart. The uplifted, expansive feeling it creates is a good example of what helps keep my energy vibration high.]*

Personal Reflections

This lesson was a communing with nature inspired by the winter scene from our kitchen window. A reminder that inner peace and stillness are not fostered by talking or words; they are felt and experienced. What a peaceful, inspiring way to begin the last day of November, 2006.

When I was growing up in rural Michigan, snow days were a cause for celebration, a rare treat. Not only were they an unexpected day off from school, they were play days. We rolled all sizes of snowballs to build snowmen, igloos, and forts. We piled on toboggans, sleds, skis, or flying saucers and went up and down the nearby hills until we were as cold as the ice crystals attached to our clothes and hair. Dragging ourselves home, happy with fatigue and hunger, we knew there was nothing better than shedding our wet snowsuits and clunky boots before coming into the warm house filled with smells of freshly baked bread and apple pie.

Fear Weaves its Web

12/5/06, 7:30 a.m., Lesson Twenty-Five

I feel your weariness and struggle to persist with staying caught up with paperwork and your readiness to be finished with the seemingly never-ending administrative work associated with your psychology practice. I also feel your fear of losing your motivation to continue writing after you close your clinical practice.

Your struggle and weariness are not a realistic picture of what's ahead nor is your fear of not using your time meaningfully after retirement. These negative, fearful, critical thoughts are in response to your perceived procrastination in completing office paperwork. You recognize your wish to avoid administrative paperwork, but you are in fact getting it done, though perhaps not without the internal push to get it done sooner and faster.

You're in the final stretch before your transition to retirement. Part of you is resisting the change because it's new and unfamiliar, and part of you is ready to move on but fearful of the unknown. This is normal, as you already know, and likely to become even more evident as this transition nears. Part of you is sad about your readiness to leave your career and professional work. Your readiness is simply an indication you have learned and done what was needed during this phase of your life. You are now ready to pursue new goals and purposes. That is positive. You will use all you've learned throughout your professional life in the endeavors that unfold in the months and years ahead. *[My teacher's detached realism and optimism in viewing my retirement is refreshingly down to earth. It helps remind me that such transitions signify readiness to move on to new purposes, new learning.]*

You fear a loss of status in others' eyes with this transition. Let that go. It's unimportant. Your view and assessment of yourself, along with your choices to follow your heart and your best understanding of your life's purpose, are what matter. No one is more or less than another in importance. We are all equal in value as souls. We are all sparks of the Universal Light working toward our return to the Divine One. Do not let your struggle, ambivalence, weariness, or fears distress you. Notice them, be aware you are not your feelings, whether they are positive or negative, and allow them to release as you keep your eye and heart-mind focused on your goals of fulfilling the spiritual purposes for which you are here. This is what matters.

Do not allow yourself to get pulled into the quicksand of doubts, fears, weariness, struggle, and procrastination. These are impermanent like everything in physical life.

Keep your heart-mind focused on the bigger picture—that you are spirit in physical form with lessons to learn and purposes to fulfill through your physical life on earth.

Periods of emotional struggle and pain are lessons and opportunities to become stronger and rise above physical life challenges. Remember the bigger picture instead of mistakenly identifying who and what you are with any particular life circumstance. The struggles and challenges inherent in physical life on earth are part of the reason it is one of the best schools of learning. Applying the lessons learned along the way is part of the challenge, particularly at times of change and uncertainty. Use this transition to keep applying learned lessons to yourself, your life, and your relationships with others.

Personal Reflections

Today's lesson reminded me how much of my personal identity is wrapped up in my profession. Since this is who I have been for more than half my lifetime, it's difficult to imagine what life will be like without my career. The only thing I'm certain about is that I will not miss the paperwork. But, just in case I've misjudged that, it's good to know there is an endless supply of that in other parts of my life! Making silly jokes and laughing help me lighten up.

I've been as honest as I can in examining what is solidly in place to help see me through this transition—support of my family and friends; a variety of meaningful activities and good health habits; my strong interest in continuing to learn new things, helping others, and fostering spiritual growth; and my excitement and curiosity about the new learning opportunities ahead. My beginning to write in the months preceding my retirement also gave me a creative outlet, a new direction.

My readiness to let go of my life's vocation and move on to other work has surprised me. I notice strong societal tendencies to value people based on material acquisitions or visible accomplishments and wonder if I will be valued less after retirement. What a relief to be reminded that others' and our social conditioning do not determine my value nor is value defined by outer criteria like work. Unless, of course, I relinquish this power to others by blindly accepting external definitions of worth. I like the concept that, as souls, we are of equal value and importance. Staying true to who and what I am and my unique purposes here is what matters. That is up to me.

LESSON
TWENTY-SIX

Perseveration on Doubts and Fears

12/6/06, 7:30 a.m., Lesson Twenty-Six

I am here with you. You can sense my presence from your heart center. That is not necessary, but it's helpful in keeping your focus and reducing your doubts. Yes, admit it. You still have doubts and you continue to wonder if you're making this up. There's no need to apologize for your doubts and questioning. It's simply the way it is and it's better to acknowledge the truth of your feelings. You fear others' contempt or ridicule and the associated loss of face if others dislike what you've written. And yet you continue to show up and write; what a paradox! That you would risk others' potential ridicule and any loss of face suggests that a deeper part of yourself believes this communication with the world of spirit is not only possible but happening. Trust this process and the part of yourself that knows it is possible and happening.

Remember, it's not your responsibility to persuade others to believe or be open to the possibility. Each person can and will decide for himself or herself. If a reaction of contempt or ridicule is possible, then it's also possible some people will sense whatever truths are inherent in these lessons and be encouraged or uplifted by it. You are often reminding your patients that what we fear has to be faced to overcome or master the fear. Remember, truths that apply to others apply to you as well *[said humorously]*. And you will never know how others respond if you don't put it out there. You correctly recognize that you're starting to drag your feet and have doubts about whether this is something you should publish. In other words, you're afraid others won't like it, will think less of you, or will make fun of you.

What about you? Will you lose esteem for yourself if you publish something that may not meet with others' approval? Or will you lose esteem for yourself if you behave like a coward and hide your work out of fear? I'm saying this in such a strong way because that's what you're thinking and feeling—that it would be giving in to fear and behaving like a coward to avoid trying to publish this as you agreed and still wish to do. *[I was indeed thinking that not following through with publishing Lessons would be cowardly.]*

Let others decide if it's helpful to them or not. In all likelihood it will be like most things: some will be open to and benefit from what they learn by reading this and others will not. That is free will. Just do your part.

Personal Reflections

It's amazing the variety of forms in which doubt and fear recirculate. As I reread today's lesson while transcribing it, I just wanted to say get over it and move on already. Recognizing the drama I created with moving back into this negative pattern of doubt and fear was a comic relief. It's so much easier to see this from the perspective of several months later.

Good lessons to remember during times of doubt: do not take myself so seriously; I am not my feelings; it will pass or change as does everything; I am not alone—every human being has similar times of doubt, uncertainty, and fear; decide what's important to me then do it without apology; don't get attached to others' approval.

My inner teacher's humorous way of reminding me to practice what I teach helped me laugh and look at things in a more lighthearted way. Like everyone, I need to find and use my courage when I'm afraid. I need to follow through with what I know to be important even when it means facing my fears about doing so. This matters immensely.

LESSON TWENTY-SEVEN

Without Change There Is No Growth

12/7/2006, 7:30 a.m., Lesson Twenty-Seven

I feel your sadness. The uncertainty and fear underneath it are temporary. I am here to comfort and reassure you. All is well and as it should be. There is nothing to fear. Uncertainty, sadness, and very often fear are inherent in the process of change. These are normal reactions to the ending of a career that is familiar and loved. Although this is now the beginning of a new and exciting phase of your life, it is as yet uncharted. It is the unknown that frightens you. There is the fear that you are not up to the task, much less managing this transition in a meaningful way. Not knowing what's ahead leaves you tense, anxious, and irritable. Does it help to know that you are not alone? Millions have made similar transitions. Everyone has to navigate the process of change—wanted and unwanted—because it's a basic law of life that all things change. Without change there is no growth.

You have experienced many changes in your life and are now at a point where you understand more fully that <u>how</u> <u>you</u> <u>respond</u> <u>to</u> and move through the changes is something you have control over. You can choose to observe, examine, and release the changing mix of feelings. You veer from sadness to uncertainty, fear, irritation, excitement, and then are completely awash in anxiety. Remember, these are all temporary and impermanent. And most important, feelings do not define who and what you are.

You have the skills to handle this transition. And you are neither alone nor forgotten. We are here to guide, assist, and support you. We are never unavailable. To belabor the point, we are never late, too sleepy, hung over, sick, or in need of a break from you and the intensity of your life on earth. We are not bound by time or space in our world of spirit so there are no limits to our being available to provide whatever assistance is needed at any time. All that's required is that you ask for our help. Your willing invitation of our help is necessary so we do not interfere with your free will to handle your life lessons and challenges as you choose. Our help—when requested—knows no limits. You may not get the answer or input you like or expect, but you can trust that it will be for your highest good. Our job is to foster your spiritual growth, to help you fulfill your life purposes on earth. *[I am struck by my inner teacher's incredible patience and nonjudgment in the face of my recurring angst. I am grateful for this model of loving acceptance and assurance that all is well and that help is available anytime for the asking. The problem is that when I get stuck in fear I have closed my heart and created a low vibration energy field that leaves me feeling separate and adrift. So I forget to ask for the help always present. Fortunately, simple things happening throughout the day will often remind me I'm not alone; they bring me back to a more cheerful outlook. Usually, it's something positive that is heart opening—reading something inspiring; children playing, laughing; smiles of strangers; the beauty of wildflowers and snowflakes; admiration of the paraplegic man going for an outing in his wheelchair; helping someone else; being with family and friends. And, regardless of the circumstances, I always receive a balanced perspective that is unfailingly helpful when I connect with my higher Self through intuitive journaling.]*

Personal Reflections

As I wrote this lesson, I recognized the truth of what was conveyed. As a result, I felt lighter, more confident of managing whatever is here and ahead.

Though these intermittent, recurring bouts of fear, sadness, and uncertainty may be a normal response to the changes that go along with adjustment to approaching retirement, I also recognize how irrational the negative thoughts are that underlie these feelings. I remind myself I have effectively managed much more challenging changes than this, and I can choose to maintain an attitude of openness and curiosity about what's ahead.

I am amazed by yet another example of how powerful thoughts are. I can focus on low energy vibration negative feelings like fear and generate more misery for myself or choose to focus on high energy vibration heart-centered feelings and create an assured inner experience. Though I absolutely know this to be true, practicing it with awareness throughout the day is still challenging. The most enjoyable way for me to practice this directly is to focus on communicating something positive in every interaction—it might be something nonverbal like a smile to acknowledge someone, a hug for a discouraged or ill friend, a genuine compliment, and honest appreciation. The simple act of saying or doing something positive and genuine is extremely powerful. When people do this with me, I notice I want to repeat it with others. Positive actions are as contagious as negative ones and they leave everyone feeling better.

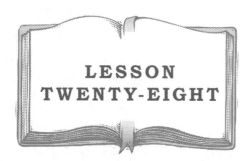

LESSON TWENTY-EIGHT

We Create Stress or Calm with our Thoughts

12/11/2006 7:30 a.m., Lesson Twenty-Eight

I feel the intense pressure you're putting on yourself in response to everything you need to do today. You fear you won't get everything done and won't be as prepared as you'd like for your meeting to begin the treatment transfer process of several patients to their new therapist.

I can feel you beginning to calm as you observe and examine the intensity of pressure you're creating by your anxious thoughts. Just as you teach your patients, the point at which you observe and are aware of an irrational response to something is the very moment you have the opportunity to choose a different, constructive response. I see your choice to relax around your goals for today and simply resolve to do your best. Prioritize the things that need to be accomplished, use the time you've allotted to prepare, then trust the process. No one will be harmed if everything doesn't get done. Visualize yourself being present to whatever you're doing. See the task flowing smoothly in an easy, relaxed manner. Begin where you are. There will be more time for meetings with the other therapists who will be continuing treatment with your patients. Be flexible in rearranging your schedule to fit in everything that's essential.

Remember—enjoy the process. Everything will eventually get done. You've never failed to complete things that are important. No matter the amount of work, enjoy the process and let go of the outcome. Then you will have done your best.

You're unnecessarily creating stress for yourself over preparations for transferring patient care because it's new and unfamiliar and you want it to go smoothly, perfectly. So far it's going very well, so trust that it will continue so. Trust the past work, planning, and preparation you've done and enjoy the process of experiencing it all. Simply see it through along with other day-to-day tasks. Repeat the process of observing your intensity and stress, releasing it, and replacing it with a more helpful, realistic response whenever you get caught up in negative thoughts that it would be awful if you didn't complete some plan perfectly. Be present to what's in front of you one thing at a time. *[I could feel my muscle tightness and inner tension settle down as I responded to my inner teacher's calm, helpful reminders. Shifting my focus to enjoying the present task helped me create a lighter attitude. There is something incredibly powerful in observing my self-defeating thoughts.*

This is the moment of choice to change course to something more positive or to stay stuck in a self-created negative spiral. This lesson brought home to me once again the power of thoughts for creating stress and negativity or calm and optimism. It also was a reminder of the benefits of meditation. The process of observing and releasing distractions to return to the chosen focus in meditation is similar to what I was reminded to do in today's lesson.]

Personal Reflections

As today's lesson pointed out, I was indeed unwittingly creating intense pressure and stress for myself by responding to my busy schedule with thoughts that I'd never get everything done and that failure to do so would be terrible. It was delightful to see again how simply observing this allowed the intensity to release. I could relax around a busy day and stay present to the task in front of me. It was easier, after that shift, to allow and accept the possibility of not completing everything without making that a catastrophe.

Changing to a more realistic view of completing a busy day's work was helpful. Taking time to alter my stressful thoughts eased the load. I was able to let go of the escalating intensity of my negative thoughts that were looping like a stuck record. If I had chosen to stay in that negative cycle, I would have continued creating a high level of stress with its detrimental effects of fatigue, reduced efficiency, and difficulty thinking clearly.

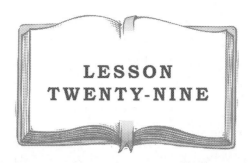

LESSON
TWENTY-NINE

Listening from
an Open Heart

12/13/2006, 7:30 a.m., Lesson Twenty-Nine

It is much easier to communicate with you when you deliberately open your heart and mind to listening and receiving. When you are caught up in the activities and stuff of physical life, your heart is less open to your connection with us. It is more difficult for you to connect with our guidance at those times because we first need to get your attention.

When you approach your daily activities and responsibilities with the intention of staying open and connected to guidance from spirit, there is a sense of lightness, curiosity, partnership, and support as you face and manage all the daily details of physical life. This is difficult to do but, as with anything, it gets easier with practice.

Your sense of feeling burdened by life's challenges dissipates when you are able to stay open to your connection with spirit throughout the day. The ways you are most likely to use for consciously keeping this open connection are through focusing on the ajna center between the eyebrows or on the heart center.

In response to your mental question, yes, there are other things you practice that also strengthen this connection. Even though you've heard them before, they are always worth repeating: meditation, diaphragmatic breathing, transformative breath exercises, guided imagery, sending positive thoughts or prayers for others. This intuitive journaling also strengthens your connection with the world of spirit and universal consciousness. This is the purpose of life in physical matter: to reconnect with Divine Source, in whatever form you conceive this to be, and to manifest the spirit of the Divine in all of daily life.

This is difficult for all of you to do for a number of reasons. Some humans are not yet awakened to the knowing that you are more than a physical body. Some people's choices make it difficult to function constructively in physical life and they get stuck in addictions of all kinds. Some lose hope and give up in the face of daunting challenges. All of you are negatively affected by fear—it is the main culprit that underlies your struggles. It interferes with your connection with spirit and its quality of unconditional love.

Earnest endeavor is very important, as is intention and taking responsibility for your own thoughts, behavior, and actions. Since life in physical is imperfect, your intention and will toward right thinking, right behavior, and right action are of most importance. Giving up on change or improvement of yourself will guarantee being stuck—you will not learn the lessons needed from physical life and you will fail to grow spiritually. The world of spirit can guide and assist you if you ask and allow yourself to be open to this. Your asking for assistance or guidance is necessary to insure there is no infringement of your free choice in all things. This is the essence of taking responsibility for yourself and your own growth.

Growth, or lack thereof, in physical life carries over to life in spirit where opportunities for learning and growth continue. There too, your free will and choice direct your continued growth and learning or remaining stuck in negative patterns, feelings, and addictions. Since there is no time or space in spirit, there is no pressure or schedule to work faster than you choose or are able with your level of spiritual development at that time. Help, support, and guidance are always available in the world of spirit and open to any who ask.

Personal Reflections

I noticed today's meditation prior to writing was more focused, less scattered than yesterday. I realized the level of tension I was experiencing yesterday blocked my openness to listening from a calm center. As a result, I was exerting effort with writing instead of allowing the words to flow. More often than not, when I'm completely in tune, I feel a sense of openness and the words come to me without effort. Yesterday, when I was blocked and distracted by tension, I did not trust that I would be able to access inner wisdom with intuitive journaling. Instead, I simply wrote using morning pages as a way of letting go of the tension and pressure I was experiencing. This had a calming effect and I ended up being very productive and calm throughout a busy day. I see now that I let my doubt interfere with using intuitive journaling despite my tension. The goal to which I aspire is to consistently maintain a calm, centered, grounded feeling in the midst of stressful circumstances anywhere.

I was intrigued by my inner teacher's comments about the carryover of our lessons and growth from life in the physical dimension to the spiritual dimension. Whatever progress or staying stuck we create here in physical life we carry with us into spiritual life when our physical bodies die. There is an elegant simplicity in this concept that growth and lessons in spiritual life pick up where we left off in physical life.

Why work so hard on our lessons in physical life, you might wonder, when we'll be continuing this work in spirit, after death of the physical body, where we imagine such work will be easier? My inner teacher says this is a matter of choice and free will for each of us. Regardless of whether we are in spirit or physical form, our essential nature is the same—we are souls in the process of evolving our consciousness toward return to Divine Oneness. From my perspective, choosing to actively participate in my growth constitutes right use of free will and choice to facilitate my soul's spiritual evolution and expression within physical matter and the greater universal consciousness.

In the soul's incarnation in dualistic physical life on earth, this process of reawakening to our divine essence and purpose necessitates a transformation of consciousness. It requires a willingness to honestly examine our entrenched, incorrect identification of who we are and our purpose with the physical body and the material world. This misidentification has left us lost to the true meaning of our soul's incarnation in physical life: to awaken to the knowledge of our divine nature as eternal souls, and to learn to express the soul's inherent qualities of unconditional love and goodwill in all aspects of life on earth. As my inner teacher pointed out in lesson three, oneness with universal love is the natural state of the spirit. Our souls patiently persist in guiding us back to the awareness that we are one with universal love.

LESSON THIRTY

Facing Fears Empowers Us

12/14/2006 7:30 a.m., Lesson Thirty

You have resisted writing this morning because your fear has once again increased. Your uncertainties and doubts about yourself increase your tension and you subconsciously revert to an attitude of steeling yourself to face the demands of the day. Your lack of trust in your own abilities and your difficulty in going with the flow, trusting all will be well, shows up as resistance to writing. Your fears and doubts get generalized to the process of writing and you approach it as if you're alone in this and it's all up to you. You fear failing to live up to the high expectations you hold for yourself.

The attitude that you are alone is false. It's a distortion that comes out of fear of not being good enough. In truth, you are never alone.

This is a joint partnership. Your commitment is to show up regularly, open your heart and mind to help from us, spirit; then transcribe the words that flow after getting your ego out of the way; and, finally, to trust this process. Our part is to stay present, provide assistance and guidance as you've asked, and trust you to do your part to the best of your ability. This is working. We're glad you showed up today despite your fears and resistance.

Yes, in response to your mental question, it's important to show up and keep on with following through with commitments whether we're open and willing or closed and resistant; relaxed and trusting or fearful and tense; feeling alone and disconnected or feeling connected with something greater. It's important to face your fears and do what's needed because that's how you will learn that you can function with fear. Not only will your fear diminish but you end up stronger, empowered, and confident.

It's also important to observe your fears and the resistance that fear creates in you. This is honest self-reflection that is necessary if you're going to choose a response other than fear and the avoidance and opposition it creates. Your growth depends on your willingness to observe your fears and, without judgment, using that moment of awareness to make a conscious choice about whether to keep avoiding or whether to move through the fear.

Because each soul comes into physical life with unique goals and contributions to fulfill, the preparation for facing fear on a day-to-day basis is important. Acknowledging and facing your myriad fears throughout the day is critical to fulfilling what you came here to do. You have had a firsthand experience of how this works. Today, by noticing your fear and resistance to writing, but doing it anyway, you have benefited. You are stronger than you were when you woke up.

Personal Reflections

The theme of fear shows up repeatedly even when I'm not consciously aware of it, like today. It shows up in a multitude of ways: tension, anxiety, worry; comparison of self with others; judgmental and critical behavior; jealousy; approval seeking; unassertive behavior; pretending; feeling unworthy; complaining; self-pity; resentment and anger, to name a few.

I was pleasantly surprised at how positive and freeing it felt to write when I didn't want to. I discovered what was hidden beneath today's wish to avoid something I usually find rewarding. Taking time to explore the reasons for resisting what I normally love and benefit from is always revealing and worthwhile in the ongoing process of knowing self.

Looking more closely and honestly, I see how self-defeating avoidance has been in my life. One way this shows up for me is putting off paperwork with excuses such as I don't feel like it even though I know I would feel much less stressed to have at least some of it completed. Another is avoiding exercise with the excuse of fatigue despite knowing I'd be more relaxed and energized with exercise. Or excusing poor eating habits, junk food, or a dessert I know will not benefit my body with I want it, I deserve it. These situations all boil down to whether I choose to allow the desires and wants of my ego self to be in charge or that higher part of Self that always encourages me toward the highest good. When I avoid making the best, healthiest choice and give in to the desires and wants of the ego self, I interfere with my soul's growth and progress. When I honestly acknowledge the self-defeating aspects of my passing ego desires and rightly use my will to choose what I know to be best, from my higher Self, I am empowered. This is true growth one small victory at a time. I'm more energized and happier when I choose wisely from the higher Self.

LESSON THIRTY-ONE

I Am Present in all Things

12/19/2006 8:00 p.m., Lesson Thirty-One

I am here with you. Look for me always in the beauty around you and within you. I am present in the bright Christmas lights you love to look at. I am the peace and warmth you feel in your heart when you look at their glow. I am the smile of pleasure that comes unbidden to your lips and eyes as you forget yourself in my light and colors. I am the joy of this season of life where you celebrate the birth of the Holy One in physical form. I am the smile of the baby that brings a warm glow to your heart and an answering smile. I am the curious, playful child who delights in your attention to their joy. I am the warmth within the cold; the light that shines in the darkness. I am the perfection of the snowflake; its white purity and crystal design have been arranged by me. I am the beauty of the soothing sound of music that moves your heart, beckoning you to look for me within. I can be found in the rhythmic beauty of your heart and the wonder of your physical body whose organs do their work without being asked, prompted, or thanked. The awesome perfection and coordination of all are my manifestations, gifted to you to remind you I am here and await your return home to me. Come to me within the stillness of your heart. There you will find the rest and peace you seek. *[I intuitively understood that the reference to returning home meant our individual and collective journey toward reunion with Divine Oneness. As I wrote as quickly as I could, I had a felt glimpse of this Oneness within. It's what I would call a sacred moment where I felt the complete goodness and oneness of life.]*

Personal Reflections

Today's lesson was written following an evening meditation. Despite my previous conclusion that writing is best done in the morning, tonight was an exception. The journaling flowed so smoothly that it felt effortless. Perhaps one's state of mind is more important to the flow of writing than the time of day. Tonight's meditation helped quiet my mind's chatter, so listening with an open heart-mind was easier. I'm also noticing the value of two things— maintaining an attitude of open curiosity to receiving whatever comes and letting go of any need to control the outcome.

The pervasive, loving warmth and peacefulness conveyed in tonight's lesson were so strong they seemed palpable.

Each rereading of this lesson puts me in touch once again with the sense of sacredness and joy inherent in this lesson. And, just think, this is always available within each of us through our connection and communication with our inner Divine essence, the higher Self. As hard as it may be to believe, these inner qualities of the higher Self and its innate wisdom can be accessed by any of us through intention and choice.

The Soul Speaks to Us through Nature

12/20/2006 10:00 a.m., Lesson Thirty-Two

You look out at today's blizzard from your kitchen window and see the snow coming down sideways and blown about by the wind. The sky and mountains are not visible. In fact, you can't see more than 1/16th of a mile in any direction because of the low hanging front that shrouds everything from earth to sky. It's as if a screen has been pulled down, but you still can see and sense the aliveness of the snow.

Your soul speaks to you through nature. At this moment, it speaks to you through the peaceful quiet and stillness of a winter day where everything is covered in pure white. The snowflakes continue to drift down, floating, each one a unique crystal, bringing moisture to the earth as well as a deep feeling of peace and contentment.

The snow is a gift from the Creator. It replenishes supplies of water. It cleanses and washes away debris. It provides the variation of seasons. It is art and beauty in nature. It provides an opportunity for rest and nourishment to earth's soil, trees, and humans. Even the gentle falling motion of the snow is soothing. It encourages you to stay indoors together and play, taking a break offered by nature from your hectic pace. The motion of the snow and the screening out of your surroundings by the blanket of snow-filled clouds has a calming effect. Think of it. There has never been a snowstorm exactly like this one. It's a one-of-a-kind winter landscape original. Enjoy it. *[I had not looked at snowstorms in this light before—one-of-a-kind originals, never duplicated, and an opportunity to shift into a slower pace, coaxed into calmness by the rhythmic motion of falling snowflakes. There's no question about getting out. It's clearly an inside day, a nature-enforced quiet time from our usual rush. What a treasure to have this unexpected respite.]*

Personal Reflections

Today's blowing snow and winter storm is a beautiful, calming sight. As I'm writing today's lesson the realization strikes me that just as the blanket of snow narrows and limits what we can see during a storm, so too the veil of invisibility between the planes of consciousness of physical and spirit limits what I see. Just because I can't see something with my physical eyes doesn't mean it's not there or has no impact on me.

The Sun Is always Present

12/22/2006, 8:40 a.m., Lesson Thirty-Three

Enjoy the sunshine after the storm. That is an apt description for much of life: a recurring cycle of small and sometimes huge storms, challenges, or adversity followed by periods of relative calm and sunny days.

The opportunities for growth most often occur during times of challenge. It is easier to be happy, focused, calm, and caring toward others when things are going well in your life. When adversity strikes—short or lengthy, small or huge, immediate and temporary or chronic and long-lasting—those are the times your resolve is tested. The opportunities for strengthening one's self and applying spiritual values are greatest at such times. Will you succumb to fear some or all of the time? Are you aware of and in charge of your fears at such times or not? Are you able to function with courage and love or do you give in to your fear? Does your heart stay open or close in fear? Do you keep your focus on the light shining through the darkness to guide you? Or do you lose your way and become ungrounded and lost? Do you remain optimistic that the sunshine will return? Or do you give up in the face of the very challenges from which you are meant to learn and grow? Do you curse the storms or accept them as part of life's lessons? *[The choices I make about how I respond to all life circumstances affect the degree of growth I make in any given situation. If I stay stuck in blaming others or external circumstances, I interfere with my being able to correct the problem and therefore limit my learning and growth. On the other hand, if I honestly acknowledge that I am in charge of my response to all happenings in my life, I am open to the growth potential they offer. The one thing I can always change is my thoughts or my response. I can change self-defeating responses to positive and empowering ones.]*

Remember always, you are never alone during the storms nor during times of sunshine. We are always here for you. You are never forgotten even though your fear during the storms of life may leave you feeling alone and forsaken, wondering why this particular adversity or challenge has come into your life. We are the light shining through the darkness to keep you certain the sun's light will again fill your life. *[What a priceless gift, this knowing I am never alone, even during the darkest times I create for myself. My higher Self is always looking out for what is best for my growth, bringing opportunities to learn new ways to transform whatever darkness my ego self may have created into something light and growth-enhancing. I am beginning to grasp more clearly at a deeper level the reality that has been in front of me all along—that I create my internal storms, fears, aloneness, and resulting unhappiness through my choices. When my ego self chooses fearful, angry, or limiting thoughts in response to life circumstances, I create the internal suffering and unhappiness that result. If I acknowledge my inherent power to choose my own thoughts and response at any given moment, then it stands to reason I can always choose a response that either limits or expands my light and growth.]*

Personal Reflections

Today's lesson using sunshine and storms as metaphors for life was written after two days of blizzard severe enough to close down most of the city. Today the sun shone. It was as welcome as the snow when it first arrived. When we're in the midst of a storm, whether its weather or upheavals in our lives, it's often difficult to remember that the sunshine is still present and will eventually become visible again. This is particularly true during times of ongoing extreme duress or when we experience one difficulty after another.

These times of stress offer the most potential for learning about self and others as well as our connection to something greater than self, whatever we believe that to be. It prods us to examine the eternal questions we all come up against: Who am I? Why am I here? What am I to learn from life? Such times of adversity offer vast opportunities for growth that will transform us in some way.

For me as well as for many of my patients, discovery of the magnitude of one's courage in facing life altering challenges is a priceless gift. I have heard others describe profound positive growth as a result of their response to personal misfortune: developing newly discovered inner strengths and talents that surfaced in the process of facing a serious health challenge; deepening one's spiritual awareness and connection; experiencing the freeing power of acceptance, forgiveness, and letting go of negative thinking; being present to each moment with an attitude of gratitude; listening to what the body is communicating with its symptoms and working along with the body's efforts to restore balance and harmony; being more loving and compassionate toward self and others; improving self-care, positive communication skills, and closeness in relationships; learning to say no and setting healthy limits and boundaries with others; releasing the harmful effects of blaming others or holding on to past hurt and resentment; developing greater clarity about what is meaningful and living from that.

Nothing Is too Mundane for Spirit

12/31/2006 8:00 a.m., Lesson Thirty-Four

What has kept you away? Perhaps you've seen your recent activities as too small or insignificant to learn or gain anything from at this time. So you have isolated yourself to take care of these matters by yourself, thinking we have better things to do than help with things you're labeling as unimportant. *[This was a concise, accurate summary of my thoughts and attitude.]*

There is nothing too inconsequential for us. Many times, the things you label mundane have far-reaching effects. Please don't shut us out because of your mistaken idea that some routine activity is too small to request our time and help. On the other hand, asking for our assistance and guidance is your choice. We are a bridge, a connection to the light of the world of spirit which is pure, unconditional love. As such, your contact with us is another way to develop and strengthen your spiritual light within. Inviting our involvement and assistance with your activities also allows us to manifest our purpose in spirit. *[This is another example of the interdependence of all things. Just as this intuitive communication benefits my growth, it also is an opportunity for my teacher to express her purpose in spirit.]*

In response to the guilt you are now feeling for letting so many days go without communicating, there is no need for it. We want you to open yourself to our guidance because <u>you</u> choose to do so and benefit from it, not because it allows us to fulfill some purpose of ours. In response to your mental question, keeping us present and seeking our guidance with intention does not mean you need to be constantly thinking or actively doing something like this to connect with us. You can relax, sleep, write, do chores, and engage in activities—we are still here. We continue to guide anyway on many levels of which you are unaware.

You can open your heart-mind to our help and guidance by focusing your awareness on either your heart center or the ajna center (between the eyebrows). *[My teacher is giving me a specific, intentional way for opening my heart-mind to inner guidance at nonwriting times throughout the day.]*

You are so used to thinking of yourself as a self-contained individual separate from others that you have not yet grasped the truth that your notion of separateness is an illusion. Maintaining your incorrect belief in your separateness from others and us <u>blocks</u> your awareness of and accessibility to us, your helpers in spirit. In truth, all is one. You, along with everyone and everything else, are part of the whole, the Light. Just as individual waves of the ocean join with the whole, you too are uniquely you yet part of the whole as are we. When you connect with us by opening your heart-mind, we are working from the whole, the world of spirit where the light of unconditional love is manifest. *[After rereading this lesson several times during editing, I realized that while I refer to my inner teacher, she refers to herself throughout this lesson as "we," "us," or "helpers in spirit." This occurred a few times in earlier sessions as well. I didn't notice it at the time of this lesson so did not ask what it meant. It seems to imply that there is more than one teacher or helper. I like the concept that our working partnership is mutually beneficial in supporting our respective spiritual growth and purposes.]*

Personal Reflections

I have avoided intuitive writing for the last nine days. I used morning pages journaling to sort through the personal issues and stresses associated with goodbyes to patients and closing my clinical practice. I have also been inundated with various housecleaning and administrative chores at work and home as well as holiday busyness. I viewed these activities as too mundane to connect with my inner teacher.

Resuming this communication with my inner teacher felt positive and I benefited from the resulting intuitive lessons today. In particular, it was helpful to be reminded that my sense of being separate from the whole blocks my connection with my higher Self and helpers in the world of spirit.

The ending of treatment relationships with patients and transition of ongoing patients to other therapists have been intense but have gone relatively smoothly. The snowstorms that closed our city for two days created a few memorable complications in rescheduling final appointments. In the end, my final day as a practicing psychologist on December 27 was much like any other except for the awareness that this was the last time I would see patients in treatment as a clinical psychologist.

What has been learned in the working relationship with each of them will have a lasting impact on their lives as well as mine. Teaching and learning are intertwined in all relationships. I'm grateful to have had this opportunity to say goodbye face to face with all my patients, for their trusting me to help and guide them, and for all I learned from each of them.

If, as this lesson indicates, inner guidance is available and operating even when we are unaware of its presence, what is the value of using intuitive writing to seek information and help? The key, it seems to me, is the expanded awareness and consciously chosen growth that intuitive journaling offers. It is a way of befriending my higher Self and directly experiencing its unconditional love. Choosing to strengthen my alignment, communication, and cooperation with my higher Self enables this deeply personal, loving relationship with my divine essence to guide my expression of love in the physical world. This purposeful relationship with my higher Self engages my free will in participating fully in my unfolding soul growth and expressing its inherent qualities of love, peace, joy, and service in the world.

LESSON
THIRTY-FIVE

New Ways to Work with Old Patterns

1/1/2007, 3:00 p.m., Lesson Thirty-Five

It's a new beginning—a new year, a new moment, a new day, a new lesson—new opportunities await. You were hesitant to write today. Since it's midday, you assumed your mind and emotions would be cluttered and interfere with listening to the intuitive information. There is some static present, but your openness and receptivity will sustain our communication. *[This static, created by my negative emotional state, refers to the slight interference I experienced today in receiving the intuitive information. Listening with my inner senses is more difficult with the distraction and energetic upheaval from negative feelings. I imagine it's like the beginning static on my car radio that tells me there is something interfering with a clear, sustained signal to my favorite music station. My teacher's choice of the word static to describe this interference was both perceptive and inventive.]*

Your current resentment toward someone you love for not helping in the way you wanted and expected with a major project is creating the static. This presents an opportunity to again let go of imposing your expectations on others. It also allows you to rid yourself of the mistaken idea that if others don't do as you expect, it means they don't care.

You have taught others to identify these same distortions in thinking you are now using: imposing your shoulds and your expectations on others, and personalizing others' behavior. There is some humor in this as you keep persevering with wanting what <u>you</u> want. You impose your standards and expectations on your loved one then feel mistreated, resentful, and sorry for yourself when he doesn't comply. As a result, you create suffering and misery for yourself as well as distance in your relationship.

Remember, your standards and expectations are your own. Expecting others to live up to your wants and shoulds is a sure way to create disappointment and is, in fact, an attempt to control others. Ask for what you need and want then let go of the outcome. Whether the response is yes, no, maybe, or silence, let go of your attachment to your desired outcome. Respect others' right to choose just as you want your choices respected.

Decide how much responsibility you are willing to take to live up to your own standards. If you're feeling overwhelmed with too much to do and no one to help, you can reduce your expectations, simplify the task, or ask someone else to help, even if it means hiring someone. This will give you more practice with flexibility. Ask yourself how important the task is and keep a reasonable perspective about it, simplifying whenever you can.

Solving your overwhelmed state of mind by trying to control or change others will never work. It's constructive to find ways to manage your need for help that do not corrode your relationships with others. We sense you have made an internal shift as you take in what we're reminding you of as it applies to your current distress. *[Another reference by my inner teacher to "we," implying there is more than one of them.]*

The dream fragment *[summarized below]* you asked for our help in understanding speaks to this issue: you are responding to your loved one's not helping with this project as if it's a crisis when it's not. The dream is pointing out there are natural consequences or a price to pay when you mistakenly label nonemergencies as emergencies.

The lesson of giving up the need to control others' behavior and situations is a tough and important one for you and almost everyone. Work on going with the flow and remember that the responsibility for taking care of your own needs rests with you, not others. When others choose to give help in response to your need or request, appreciate it as the gift it is.

When you ask for others' help and the response is no in whatever form, find another way to accomplish the goal if it's important to you. Modify the goal, simplify it, or break it down into manageable steps. Re-evaluate the importance of the goal or let go of needing to accomplish it in the way you wished. Recognize that most things are preferences.

There are many ways to accomplish things of importance to you. There is also a time to let go of things that are not feasible. Your well-being and happiness do not depend on controlling others into investing in what's important to you. Instead of helping with your project in the ways you wanted, your loved one built a snow-woman to celebrate you, your retirement, and the new year. How special is that!

Personal Reflections

Today's lesson relates to my longstanding, stubborn, counterproductive pattern that once again emerged during the recent holiday stress of wanting and expecting help completing a major project that was important to me.

Never mind that the ways I wanted help were not typical ways my loved one offers help; I simply ignored that reality. Though I see the humor in this now, not even a smiling thought was to be found at the time. That, of course, was a big part of the problem—my thoughts were seriously rooted in victimhood. I was reacting to not getting the help I wanted in the ways I expected. I behaved as if it were a crisis, which certainly kept my nervous system revved up and on high alert. The bottom line was that I just wanted my way.

Just in case I didn't learn what was needed from the misery I had managed to create for myself, I had a dream that also addressed this very issue, though I did not understand its meaning until today's lesson. It is clear to me now that the dream was necessary as I was not getting the message about how I was creating my own misery.

Here's a summary of the dream: I was making a 911 call to report an emergency. As the operator came on, I realized it was an emergency only in my dream and not a real life crisis so I told the operator I dialed 911 before realizing there was no real emergency. The operator in the dream was understanding but firm in telling me I'd have to pay for the dispatching of emergency personnel even though it was a mistake. I accepted that in the dream since it was my mistake that I made a 911 call based on a dream emergency. After recording the dream in my dream journal, I was still clueless about what in my current life I was reacting to as a true emergency when it was, in fact, a false emergency. So, I asked for help from my inner teacher in understanding the dream message.

The interpretation offered in today's lesson made me laugh. It captured my attention in a powerful way. The explanation made perfect sense. Without this major assistance from my inner teacher, I would not have deciphered the dream message on my own. I was too entrenched in my own self-focused perspective to see my part in the problem. The lesson, I gather, is stop trying to control things—and people.

The most powerful learnings I was reminded of from today's lesson and continue to use are these:

- I am responsible for my happiness or lack thereof and meeting my own needs and expectations.
- Happiness is an inner experience that I create or limit with my thoughts. Happiness is not dependent

on what others do or don't do—it is an internally created experience.

- When I need help from others, ask and respect their right to choose, regardless of their response. Appreciate the assistance others choose to give as well as the ways they offer it. Let go of trying to control others and outcomes.
- There is incredible power in choice. Accepting responsibility for my own choices is both freeing and necessary for my personal and spiritual growth.

Despite my initial self-created funk over having to complete the major project by myself, I paced the work and enjoyed it. Today's lesson made a huge impact and I'm sure to reap the benefits of this lesson in many future situations. It allowed me to appreciate the creative way my loved one <u>chose</u> to celebrate the beginning of my retirement and a new year by building a snow-woman in my honor. The unveiling of the snow-woman was a sweet moment, captured for perpetuity on film. To this day, the photo brings a smile to my heart. This positive, loving image never fails to remind me of today's lesson.

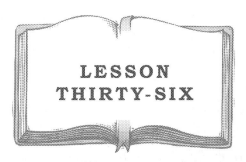

LESSON
THIRTY-SIX

Schools of Physical and Spirit Life

1/2/2007, 8:15 a.m., Lesson Thirty-Six

Though there is no time here in the world of spirit, our work is closer to what you're now experiencing with the transition to retirement. That is, we choose and pace our activities, classes, recreation, and time with others since there are no time pressures or deadlines. We do, however, have a deep level of commitment to our work in spirit. There can be a sense of urgency here, as well, in carrying out our purposes because of our awareness of how our work fits with the big picture. We have a deep desire to do our work well, and we all have purposeful work unique to each of us.

Part of our contract for fulfilling our soul's purpose and continued learning and growth is to help and guide you while you are in physical life. Yes, in response to your mental question regarding the meaning of our use of we and us, there are several of us and we have access to others in spirit if we have need of special knowledge or expertise in teaching through you. I am the leader of the group and the contact for communicating with you; that will not change. The link and manner of this communication is through intuition activated by your awareness and choice to open your heart and mind to this way of teaching. *[This is a working partnership in more ways than I imagined.]*

You are thinking of past president Gerald Ford's death *[note: he died 12/26/06]* and the legacy he has left. His humility, his not putting himself above others, and his comfort with his human ordinariness were important qualities he contributed as a leader that are positive examples for all of us. He will be missed there and welcomed back here in his ongoing work from spirit. And yes, in response to your mental question regarding whether past president Ford can go swimming here, he can swim and be as physically active as he chooses in spirit. Here, just thinking about swimming or some other enjoyed activity or place brings it about. *[This ability of the higher Self or soul to create with thought or intention when in spirit is also described in Lesson twenty-two.]*

There is no frailty, illness, or limitation of any sort in spirit. There is no war, hatred, anger, competition, jealousy, addiction, or depression in spirit. People are freed of physical afflictions when they pass over into spirit. The learning from their afflictions while in physical life affects where their learning and lessons in spirit continue. The more work done in physical form, the greater the effect on our ongoing development in spirit. It is all of a whole, all a part of the same process.

Learning and growth are part of all life whether it's in spirit or physical life. The only difference is the circumstances under which our lessons present themselves. Physical life on earth is as much a school for learning as is the world of spirit.

Our lessons, both in spirit and in physical, are individualized and perfectly geared for our current level of development on the path of awakening and enlightenment.

Personal Reflections

The luxury of being retired and able to organize my time and activities without fitting them in around my work schedule is delightful and freeing. I am continuing the morning routine I've benefited from for years: meditation, exercise of some kind, writing, and a good breakfast. I'm grateful for the daily writing habit already well-established before I retired.

Today's lesson provided a few more insights into the nature of life in spirit. For starters, those in spirit have active, purpose-filled lives without the limitations and pressure of time, wars, hatred, or other human problems. They create and communicate by thought. Unlimited opportunities for continued learning and classes, activities, interests, and time with others are available though at a more relaxed pace.

When we pass over into spirit, we are freed from any disability or illness, physical or mental, we may have had in physical form. The degree to which we have gained or learned spiritually from our physical life experience determines where our individualized learning begins in spirit. This makes perfect sense to me. It also motivates me to progress as much as possible while in physical form. I was especially intrigued by the ability in spirit to manifest or create an enjoyed activity or place simply by thinking about it.

Since I enjoy learning, I was relieved to hear about the rich variety of work that is present in spirit. Upon physical death, our soul essence returns to spirit, its natural state and home, to continue learning and evolving toward union with Divine Source.

Despite the stark differences between physical life and this description of life in spirit, both are part of the larger whole, part of the same process. In my view, this implies both are part of the universal consciousness but different vibrational expressions of the whole. In physical life, we need to awaken to the forgotten truth that we are spirit in physical form, and allow this to inform our learning and growth until we again return to spirit, our natural state, where we continue to evolve.

Why do we need to leave the world of spirit at all to learn? Why struggle here in physical form when, from my teacher's description, it seems that spirit is a more pleasant environment in which to learn? I don't know; I can only share how I make sense of this. It is my belief that our soul, guided by helpers in spirit and a universal plan of evolution that is beyond our comprehension, chooses the environment that can best provide the individualized soul lessons we need at any given point in our evolving development as spiritual beings. If incarnation in physical matter is chosen as the best learning environment, the soul guides our growth process and rediscovery of our divine essence as we learn to go within in our search for meaning and purpose. For example, the soul's inner guidance may appear as our conscience cueing us when we are acting out of alignment. The choice to listen and grow is ours. I have to admit, our dualistic physical life offers a wealth of opportunities for learning to freely choose to live from our soul nature and its natural qualities of unconditional love and peace!

From the information my inner teacher provides, those in spirit are aware of how their work and purposes fit with a greater plan. This contributes to their deep commitment to excel at fulfilling their unique purposes from spirit.

My inner teacher is apparently the leader of a group of souls in spirit who are teaching through me—this explains the occasional use of "we," "us," and "helpers in spirit" throughout the lessons. According to my teacher, our connection and communication is through intuition or the higher Self. It is activated by my awareness of my spiritual nature as well as my free choice to open my heart-mind to this way of learning.

This collaborative partnership between my inner teacher(s) from spirit and me in physical is mutually beneficial and allows all to learn and evolve through working together. I gratefully receive their guidance while in physical life and, by offering their assistance, they fulfill their soul's purpose and continue to evolve in spirit. It's still hard for me to wrap my mind around this but it provides a glimmer of how our interdependence within the whole works. I simply accept it and am grateful to be a means for spreading to others the lessons I have been given.

LESSON THIRTY-SEVEN

Practicing Stillness through Mindful Presence

1/3/2007, 9:05 a.m., Lesson Thirty-Seven

It is indeed a peaceful scene that you see before you: the beauty of pure snow-covered mountains, the green cedars and pines, the sun's light filtering through the clouds, and birds flitting from place to place.

The quiet and stillness are what you are in need of at this moment. Your mind has been too busy planning how to complete the unfinished parts of closing your practice. You're trying to focus on too many things at one time. *[This refers to after-retirement work of completing final patient reports, business and administrative details to be wrapped up in the next three months, and clearing out my office.]*

It will all get done. Break it down. Focus on one task at a time and be present with that task until it's completed to the extent possible. Let go of holding onto all the other unfinished tasks. Thinking about them simply depletes your energy, increases your feelings of internal tension, and leaves you feeling and acting rushed. Those reactions are not only unpleasant but create more stress. There's nothing so urgent that it has to be done immediately. You are skilled at prioritizing and can choose to focus only on the task in front of you. Allowing yourself to worry or feel tensely preoccupied with unfinished work still ahead of you takes away from your efficiency and productivity in completing the work in front of you.

If you look deeply at nature you can see the reflections of nature within self and the reflection of your inner self in nature. All is one energy. You and all of nature are part of the same whole. You sense the power of the single minded focus on what's present when you look out your window right now and observe the enlivened stillness and peaceful quiet of nature. To create such stillness within self, focus only on the task at hand. Set aside other tasks to wait their turn as you select where your focus needs to be.

It is possible to do several things at once but there is a cost attached. The quality and efficiency of your work is affected and, more importantly, the inner quality of your experience of the task at hand is negatively affected. Instead of clear focus, you are mentally distracted, scattered. Instead of inner quiet, you fill your mind with the chatter of worried, pressured thoughts beneath your conscious awareness. Instead of relaxed engagement with what you're doing, you tense around it. Instead of feeling energized by what you're doing, you feel depleted, rushing from one thing to another as if you're in a race against time. The race and pressured pace are created by your mind.

If you can create this kind of tension and pressure for yourself with your mind, you can do the opposite as well. You can create a sense of peace, stillness, and enjoyment by consciously staying focused only on the task at hand. Choose a mindful, noncritical focus on each task, giving it your best. You'll be less fatigued and frazzled. The cumulative tension of mentally paying attention to what's undone while you're working on another task will fade away.

Try this today. Observe the differences in your inner experience, efficiency, level of pleasure in what you're doing, and the effect on others of a pressured style versus a focused, relaxed, mindful approach to what is in front of you. *[I have been practicing this approach, especially during times I feel rushed or pressured. As I stayed with it, I got better at observing the rushed tension and the fast, shallow breathing that nearly always went with it. This reminded me how rushed thoughts and feelings induce a similar rushed, stressful breathing pattern. I began using my rushedness as a signal to slow and deepen my breath to relax. When I persisted, my thoughts and breathing calmed after a few minutes. Staying focused on the task in a more relaxed way was then easier. Even mundane chores were more enjoyable if I remembered to approach them with this mindful, relaxed focus.*

Expanding my practice of mindful focus from meditation to exercise and yoga by coordinating breath with slow stretches or movement also helped facilitate my being able to apply this approach to other situations where I was creating rushed tension and stress. Though this is an ongoing process, it is very satisfying and empowering to see signs of progress and to feel the greater centeredness and inner relaxation it produces. I have also been pleasantly surprised to see it spilling over into other areas like relationships.]

Personal Reflections

Today's lesson again used the winter nature scene as a metaphor for creating inner stillness, peace, and mindful focus on each moment. From the moments of inner stillness and clear focus I have so far experienced, I see how it helps connect with deep inner peace. At such times of being present with what is, I notice greater mental clarity and enjoyment of the task at hand as well as increased efficiency and energy. This is a powerful motivator to sustain this focused approach during stressful times where the mind becomes scattered and busily absorbed with daily concerns.

This way of being and approaching life cannot be forced or attained through effort. Rather, it seems to occur in response to an open heart-mind in the context of a nonjudgmental, relaxed attitude of acceptance of whatever is. Practice is definitely required to make it a more habitual response and to sustain this way of being. The results are well worth it. Like us, nature has many faces besides its quiet stillness and its bounty: stormy times, destructive events, upheaval, draught, and famine. The key, I suspect, is to work toward finding and maintaining an attitude of engaged stillness, doing one thing at a time in responding to all of life's challenges. Definitely easier said than done.

For me, awareness of the breath is one of the most helpful habits I have cultivated as it quickly reflects my level of tension or calm. From this awareness, it's an easy step to shift into slow deep breathing from the abdomen. It calms the body-mind so clear focus is possible. Heart-focused gratitude breathing works best for me as it simultaneously serves as a reminder to keep the heart open and appreciate the task in front of me.

LESSON THIRTY-EIGHT

Fear Creates Doubt

1/4/2007, 8:47 a.m., Lesson Thirty-Eight

I see you are still anxious about whether the words written here will be of any value to others and if they are indeed from us in spirit. Yes, the teachings are from us as received by you. Let others determine whether these teachings are of value to them or not. That is not something you can control, nor is it your concern. *[This is yet another example of how persistent the ego self is in reverting to "what if" fears. No doubt you will recognize these oft repeated fears. It is clear that recognizing and mastering fear is a major lesson for me.]*

The task you agreed to take on was to record the information that comes through in our time together and eventually publish the lessons. The rest is up to others. Remember to stay focused only on those things for which you are responsible. You are not responsible for others' response to or use of these teachings. Simply do the best you can in fulfilling what you've committed to and keep yourself healthy in body, mind, and spirit so you have the best vehicle for our communication. If you doubt and question this, it is very likely others will too. Let that go. It is expected, and others' doubts are not yours to fix.

What has happened, you are wondering, that you've begun doubting and questioning this again? Fear.

You have begun to wonder what others, especially friends and family, will think about these writings and, more importantly, what they will think of you for writing and believing them. You fear others' ridicule and loss of esteem. This is a good example of how fear undermines our commitment to doing what is right and true. Regardless of others' assessment and reactions, it is vitally important to think for yourself, be who you are, and do what you know to be right in your heart. These require courage. There will always be those who judge, criticize, disapprove, and ridicule if you stray from what they think or, more accurately, what they're willing to acknowledge to themselves and others about their beliefs.

Staying true to yourself, your purpose, and what you believe—this is most important. You are self-conscious about exposing yourself in this way because you fear being humiliated or abandoned by friends and family. The choice is this: do you give in to your fears or do you stay true to who you are and follow through with your commitment to share these lessons with others? We see you are affirming your choice to face your fears and complete this work.

You can see now, from a new perspective, the value of past experiences where you were afraid and wanted to quit, but you stuck it out and did what you feared anyway. You would not be where you are today if you had not done so, and we would not be doing this writing project together. This challenge of recording and publishing these teachings has arisen because you were able to face fears in the past. We trust you will do so this time as well. *[I'm grateful for my inner teacher's reminder that this is simply another lesson in facing and overcoming fear as well as her confidence that I'll master this fear too. Even with the directness with which this lesson is stated, it is still clear to me that the choice is wholly mine.]*

Personal Reflections

Today's lesson was a reminder of the benefits of facing past fears and the ongoing ways in which fear shows up throughout our lifetime. Successes, accomplishments, new learning, and opportunities for continuing growth are only possible if we're willing to face what we fear and be true to who we are and what we believe to be important. That involves risking others' potential disapproval, criticism, or ridicule. If I abdicate what I know to be right and important for me, I will have limited my growth and learning and allowed myself to be disempowered by fear. I am grateful for the reminder that doubts and skepticism are to be expected. But I am only responsible for my own doubts and skepticism and how I choose to respond to the underlying fear.

LESSON THIRTY-NINE

The Power of Genuine Gratitude

1/5/2007, 8:30 a.m., Lesson Thirty-Nine

Snow days like this where you're cocooned safely at home are good times to reach inward with gratitude and appreciation.

I am grateful you are willing to be my message bearer from spirit. I am grateful you are reliable and consistent in showing up for our time together. I'm grateful you take the thoughts I send mentally and write them out longhand. I admire the flow of your handwriting. I am awed by the beautiful winter scene as I see through your eyes. I thank you for arranging a peaceful and pleasant corner from which to write. The sound of the waterfall is soothing and the flowers a reminder of winter's impermanence.

I thank you for opening your heart and mind to me each day, for sharing yourself with me. I appreciate your curiosity and eagerness to learn more about my world and life in spirit. I smile at the intensity and effort you bring to this effortless task. *[I can't help but laugh—this is now like a standing joke reminding me to let go of results and outcome.]* I value your desire and intention to do this well and accurately. I like your awareness and smiling appreciation of the way I phrase things, my affectionate teasing, the kindness and humor with which I convey lessons for your growth. I am grateful you enjoy and look forward to this, that your day feels incomplete if you don't get to your writing.

I admire your work ethic, your following through with commitments, your willingness to look at and face the fears that often arise for you. I am touched by your affection for me and the respect you show toward me. I am grateful we are alike in our dedication to learning and teaching where it is requested. I value your honesty and integrity, the lack of pretense in how you operate in the world. I love the gentle and loving energy in your heart. I treasure your love of nature, flowers, and rich colors. I am appreciative of your surrounding yourself with beautiful, brightly colored decorations. I love the inspiring and uplifting music playing.

Yes, in response to your thoughts, expressing genuine gratitude and appreciation is a powerful force in relationships and everyday life. Just as the feelings in your heart center have warmed and glowed with accepting my appreciation and gratitude, so too do others when you offer genuine appreciation and positive feedback.

It is important when using positive communication skills to do so with genuineness and sincerity rather than a desire to manipulate or control others. Intention matters. Using positive communication to manipulate or control others to do what you want is negative use of such skills.

We are grateful you accept and receive our positive communications. It is as important to open your heart to honest, heartfelt positive input from others as it is to be sincere and genuine in giving positive feedback to others. You know from personal experience that relationships and interactions with others are more relaxed, open, trusting, and close when communication is honest, direct, respectful and, whenever possible, positive and appreciative. The most effective way of resolving conflicts or expressing a difference of opinion is to directly but kindly express your own thoughts without dismissing or derogating others. It is altogether more pleasant to interact in this manner and it increases the potential that others will receive what you are expressing with more openness.

Personal Reflections

I am moved and honored by this warm, powerful expression of my inner teacher's gratitude. Being on the receiving end of such heartfelt appreciation reminds me of the incredible power of genuinely expressed gratitude. It also inspires me to express this much more in my own daily interactions with others and in the form of gratitude letters. Gratitude opens my heart. Every time I move into judgment or some other negative attitude, I can reopen my closed heart by shifting to heartfelt care.

I am humbled because my part in this writing project is dwarfed by what I have gained and learned from this priceless communication with the world of spirit through alignment with my higher Self. It fosters awareness and growth of my soul and inspires me to express this in daily physical life.

LESSON
FORTY

We Are Not Our Thoughts and Feelings

1/6/2007, 2:15 p.m., Lesson Forty

You are surprised at how pleasant it is to simply observe the many different birds outside your window and their resourcefulness in finding food beneath the melting snow. Bird watching is much like people watching. It's entertaining, sometimes comical, as well as an opportunity to learn new things and be reminded of the oneness of all life. It's also a chance to marvel at the industriousness of birds and people, their resilience and adaptability, their beauty and uniqueness, and the burdens and challenges with which they all live. Appreciating nature through bird watching is peaceful. Such times of simple pleasures, unrushed, are needed to restore and revitalize yourself.

Carry this feeling of peace with you throughout the day. Observe what enhances this peaceful feeling, what distracts from it, and what diminishes it. See if you can allow it to stay as strongly present even in circumstances that elicit nonpeaceful feelings. Do this without judgment. Just observe and focus on restoring feelings of peacefulness when there is turmoil around or within you.

Remember, you are not your feelings. Do not confuse feelings, even positive ones, with who you are.

See your feelings as they are: temporary passing experiences. Observe them and let them go. Getting attached to or holding onto a feeling, even peacefulness, is failing to recognize the reality that we are not synonymous with passing thoughts and feelings. Attempts to hold on to feelings is to resist the reality of change and the impermanence of all emotions and thoughts.

Notice the flow of your inner life, its changing scenery of feelings and thoughts, and their effects on your physical body and behavior. Just observe your inner experience of the present moment and let it go without trying to hold on to it. Notice what you get attached to and have trouble letting go of as well as what you resist and push away, avoid, or hide. These are all temporary experiences and do not define who you are.

You, your essence, are more than the personality you associate with your thoughts, feelings, beliefs, behavior, activities, work life, family life, or relationships. The eternal you, that spark of the Divine sometimes referred to as the soul, is the source of the peace you are now experiencing within your physical self.

Personal Reflections

At the time of this editing, after putting the concepts and suggestions from my inner teacher into practice for longer periods of time, I came to view feelings of inner peace as a natural result of being in alignment with my higher Self. I believe we are all searching for this connection with the unique divine light within, our souls.

Feelings of inner peace, unconditional love, gratitude, and joy give us glimpses of this connection as they are natural qualities of the higher Self. As such, they are always present and accessible to the degree we are attuned with our higher Self and our Source.

The expression of our soul essence is not stagnant but dynamic; it flows and changes. Inner peace experienced now is unique to this moment. Our recognizing its impermanence only reflects our awareness that change is a constant of life. Our next experience of inner peace will again be unique to that moment. Trying to grasp and hold onto even such positive feelings closes the heart with fear, creating a sense of separation from our higher Self. This limits the expression of our soul's light in our physical lives, just as holding onto the physical past interferes with being fully present with life as it is now. Peace and joy can be present in myriad forms when we are living from an integration of our physical ego self with our soul essence which moves with the constant change of life.

Looking at this from another perspective, becoming aware of and correcting negative thinking patterns such as self-judgment, fear, and self-hatred are also an essential part of soul growth. These negative mental habits disconnect us from our higher Self as they close our heart-mind, creating a false sense of separation from our true essence as spiritual beings.

With awareness comes the potential for change, whether it's awareness of wanting to hold onto positive feelings or awareness of the stress of negative feelings. I prefer simple ways of working with both, using variations of heart-breathing tools. When I become aware of wanting to hold onto a positive feeling like joy in a forced, unnatural way, I first tune into my breathing as it most often reflects that tension. As I slow and deepen the breath with diaphragmatic breathing, I breathe the grasping feelings into the heart's compassion and gently release them with each out breath. I silently express gratitude for the experience of the joy, an expression of my higher Self, and the reminder that I had moved into fear or grasping.

Similarly, when I become aware of nonpeaceful thoughts and feelings, I tune into my breathing and begin slow, deep breathing while focused on my heart center. Since the heart is associated with love and compassion and its spaciousness, I breathe the negative thoughts and the feelings into the heart's compassion and gently release them with each out breath. As I do this, usually a more neutral, detached, or compassionate way of viewing the situation will come to mind, and I silently express gratitude for this help from my higher Self. Of course, the times I am unaware or even choose to remain stuck in negativity,

I soon recall I have created roadblocks to my own growth from a false sense of separation from my higher Self. Even these occasions are powerful learning opportunities for compassion, acceptance of imperfection, and forgiveness.

Where You Are Is Exactly Where You Need to Be

1/7/2007, 8:30 a.m., Lesson Forty-One

You are wondering why you had such difficulty focusing your mind in meditation this morning. You expected your mind to be quiet and easily stilled. Instead, it quickly latched onto things you plan to do later in a pressured, intense way that was completely out of proportion with what needs to be done.

This anxious intensity is a general attitude with which you approach life. It's a fear-based response. You unconsciously expect criticism, disapproval, or punishment if certain things aren't done quickly so you can move on to the next important thing, whatever that might be. You are approaching your day-to-day life as if what you're doing in the present moment is of no or little value. *[Yikes! This*

184

again? I was hoping my work so far would have yielded more progress. Apparently, there's still more work to be done on this chronic, strongly conditioned, unconscious pattern. That was obvious from my eye-opening surprise at my teacher's perspective which clearly captured the difference between mindless doing and valuing each moment no matter the task. It was as if I had heard this oft repeated lesson for the first time! That suggests today's lesson is another layer of work on this entrenched pattern. Perhaps there has been some progress after all.]

Your focus on getting through one thing so you can move on to the next leaves you living in a pressured way, missing the pleasure of being fully present to what you're doing now. *[I recognize the truth of this. The times I have fully engaged my attention and presence with what is happening in that moment are times I experience clarity of mind and a timeless ease of simply going with the flow. The key, at least for me, is to expand this engaged presence with each moment to things I judge as small, simple, or unimportant. Nothing is small or unimportant.]*

You fear you are not giving or doing enough because you have a flawed view of service and giving. Everything done, thought, felt, or acted upon that is chosen freely from a connection with Source and your soul's light is service. Anything that develops the light of love in your unique way is service as it helps move you and all living things toward enlightenment, the goal of all. *[I love this expanded view of service.]*

Because you are imperfect and in physical form to learn certain lessons, you necessarily feel some press from the sense of there being too much to learn and do to return Home. This is not bad. Though it is uncomfortable and makes you question yourself, it also helps motivate you to live your life the best you can, using opportunities presented to learn, grow, and serve. The birds feeding outside your window now, for example, are serving at this moment by sustaining their physical health through satisfying their need for food which allows them to do the things that define their purpose.

You are dissatisfied with where you are in meditation and think you should be beyond the mind wandering and obsessing about unimportant things. It's more growth-enhancing to recognize and accept this without judging or evaluating it. *[I laughed at how spot on this was. Even though I was not consciously aware of it, I did hold an expectation that I should be past all the mental distractions that present themselves during meditation. A great reminder that growth flows from an attitude of noticing and accepting the presence of distractions, even signs of imperfection, without judging them or myself.]*

Where you are is not good or bad; it simply is.

Acceptance of what is when it's not where you want to be is a learning opportunity itself. Approach all things as positive learning opportunities instead of occasions to fault yourself for where you are at this moment.

Where you are is exactly where you need to be.

Rest in the acceptance of that while keeping on with putting into practice what you know. This opens further opportunities to learn and grow. That too is serving.

Personal Reflections

This kind of acceptance is a tough one for me so I work with it by reminding myself I'm exactly where I need to be when I get caught up in something negative. I ask myself what the lesson is I need to learn. So, when I revert to my pressured intensity to get more done quickly, I remind myself it will all get done, and it will be more relaxed and enjoyable if I simply focus on what I've chosen to do at that moment. When I can do this, I'm still efficient and productive but more easygoing, attentive to what I'm doing, valuing even simple tasks.

My inner teacher's expanded view of service was new to me and one I had never considered. It seems to come from a much larger perspective that is rooted in our connection with divine Source and the higher Self which are unconditional love. From this perspective, everything freely chosen that manifests and develops our soul's unique light of love is service. It contributes to the growth of all. Our choosing to express our soul's unique talents, gifts, and life purposes in human form contributes to the collective evolution of all and, as such, is service.

LESSON FORTY-TWO

All Change Begins within Us

1/8/2007, 7:30 a.m., Lesson Forty-Two

We hope, along with you, that you get all your outstanding treatment reports and letters done so your worried preoccupation with this is less of a distraction and energy drain. Just as you observed your desire to avoid writing this morning and did it anyway, do the same with your paperwork so it's finalized.

Yes, in response to your wondering if your procrastination has a deeper meaning beyond disliking paperwork, your procrastination is another way your anxiety about the future is manifesting. This putting off of reports to be completed also allows you to let go of work more gradually. Since you dislike paperwork, this was the best thing to put off because letting go of your least favorite part of work will be easier *(said with humor)*.

We see you are holding on to keeping holiday decorations up longer, too. They are bright, cheerful, and peaceful reminders of the holidays. Even so, time marches on with the new year changes in leadership and the hope that is connected with these changes.

You, and many others, feel a deep sense of hopelessness and helplessness about the current world situation and how to stop the terror of war, including religious conflict and killing, begun out of revenge, hatred, fear, or political power agendas. Do not fear. There is a reason, too, for the current state of affairs, and good can come from this. Changes in leadership will allow for new ideas and efforts to restore balance.

Violence in all its forms—the killing of war; lack of food, money, safe water, housing, education, and safety; hateful thoughts and behavior in the form of abuse, bullying, intimidation, denying basic rights and needs—is a physical manifestation of the pervasive violence in thought and behavior of collective humanity, including nations that initiate war and killing for reasons other than defense from attack. Violence in response to violence never works. It simply instills increased hate, fear, anger, rage, hopelessness, and despair which erupt into more violence. You feel hopeless because so many of the problems underlying violence seem institutionalized in attitudes and ways of behaving that preclude change.

It is not so hopeless.

Peace and freedom from violence begin within each of you. Your responsibility is to be free of violence within yourself, in your relationships, in your approach to problems in your life. Carry this with you into everything you do. If people stopped supporting companies that perpetuate or condone violence, the social force produced by this economic investment choice would be powerful.

More basic, though, is the lack of awareness that you are all one. What affects one affects everyone whether you acknowledge that reality or not.

Right thought and right behavior are a personal choice that honor the divine within, your soul's direction. The greater number of people who respond to the divine inner guidance of their souls and strive to manifest love and peace in their lives and relationships, the more that the opposing duality of hate and violence is evident. *[My teacher seems to be saying that the stronger the will toward demonstrating the soul's qualities of love and peace, the more apparent will be its opposing duality of hate.]* This represents the war within each of you. It provides opportunities to see the devastation caused by destructive choices of hatred, injustice, aggression, absence of compassion, and desire for punishment. You can choose wisely and do your part in manifesting peace, love, justice, sharing, and equality in the world.

Change begins within you and affects everyone and everything. That in itself empowers you and gives you reason to remain hopeful and actively engaged in doing your part, whatever form that takes. Be peace today and every day.

Personal Reflections

Who, in this day and age, does not worry about the state of the world and our safety in it? How can I fail to notice my own jaded hopelessness about the ability of humanity to solve its problems in ways that promote peace and fairness? We seem to have commercialized fear as if it's part of the buy more mentality. With technological advances providing us with nonstop evidence of the harm caused by mankind, it's easy to understand the worry and fear it engenders.

Yet, my inner teacher does not seem to have been affected by this contagion of fear. That alone leaves me hopeful. She offers quite a different perspective: that what we see in the world is a reflection of what is within each of us. The moment-to-moment choices we make reflect either the darkness of the physical ego's fear and separation or the light of the soul's love and compassion. This represents our own internal challenge in learning to face and master our personal and collective inner darkness.

The power of this is that the work of change and transformation of ourselves and the world are one and the same. Transforming violence to peace begins within each of us. No one can do the work for anyone else. Each positive change made by any one of us affects all of us just as our negative, fearful behavior affects all things. As we become more consciously attuned to our soul's light within and attempt to live from that alignment, the more aware we also become of our own fearful, hateful, greedy thoughts, words, and behavior that are reflected in collective humanity. This allows further opportunities to transform our own negative energy to peaceful, kind, inclusive, and loving energy.

It would seem that looking at the current state of affairs in the world from my own fearful perspective, I have once again mistakenly assumed that peace is external. In truth,

I'm looking in the wrong place for peace. My inner teacher is pointing out that I need to look within for peace. If I do not create peaceful thoughts, words, and attitudes within, how can I expect to express and experience peace in my outer world? Peace, like love and forgiveness, is an inner experience that results from living from the soul's inherent qualities. What is created within gets expressed in the outer world. This concept that we collectively create peace in our outer world as we individually create peace within ourselves in our daily choices reflects, in a profound way, the importance of each of us within the whole.

So, it's back to basics. Focus on what I have control over—changing myself. I can choose to create peace and loving kindness within myself and express that in all ways. I can ask for help in honestly looking within at my behaviors, then take responsibility for recognizing and replacing those that are unkind, blaming, or nonpeaceful with ones I know to be a true expression of my higher Self. If ever in doubt about a sincere, peaceful way of responding to any situation, I can quiet myself and ask from an open heart for the best way to respond that serves the highest good. If I'm too angry to do that, I can take a deep breath before speaking or acting and remove myself until I am calm enough to be constructive. For each moment, I aspire to live from the light of my higher Self and ask for help in thinking, speaking, and acting with kindness, peace, and care for all beings, all life.

The Power of Observing Feelings without Judgment

1/9/2007, 7:30 a.m., Lesson Forty-Three

Being anxious or uncertain is uncomfortable but usually not life threatening, as you have reminded your patients. Feeling stressed is also not synonymous with being out of control, as you are thinking at less conscious levels. It's simply uncomfortable to feel anxiety, so you resist it instead of observing and sitting with it.

Yes, you forgot about that simple, powerful coping tool, but it's the one most needed now. Try it right now. Simply sit with the most uncomfortable feeling you're having and observe it without evaluating or trying to change it. Notice what occurs spontaneously as you observe it. Can you see what happens? By facing and accepting the presence of the negative feeling and observing it, the feeling dissipated. It lost its power. Perhaps you even got some insights or ideas about what was needed at a deeper level.

Feelings are nothing to be feared. If acknowledged and listened to, they will release. That's the opposite of resistance. The natural impulse when you feel something negative or uncomfortable is to resist it in some form. You tighten around it. Your protective walls go up. You push it away, stuff it down. You ignore it or pretend it doesn't matter. You get pulled further into the feelings as if that is who you are.

You cannot learn from feeling experiences until you notice your resistance, then shift from resistance to observing and accepting the presence of the feeling. Feelings are temporary; they wax and wane. You feed negative feelings by resisting, fearing, and over-identifying with them, acting as if the feeling is you. Of course, a negative feeling will remain uncomfortable initially. Think of that as a bonus because it gives you ample opportunity to observe the feeling as it releases and to notice what it tells you about yourself.

Anytime you are consumed by a feeling, you are overly attached to it; you have identified with it. As soon as you notice your attachment to holding onto the feeling, stop and sit with the feeling wherever it is in your body and simply observe it. Notice how it shifts. Notice any resistance you may have to releasing it, and what you might get from holding onto the feeling instead of releasing it.

This is a wonderful tool for understanding yourself and detaching from feelings instead of allowing them to control you.

I repeat, you are not your feelings.

You are more than your thoughts, feelings, needs, and behavior. Let that pure essence of light that is eternally and uniquely you, your soul, guide you in this process of observing, accepting without judgment, learning from, and releasing both negative and positive feelings. They are all temporary and impermanent. It is no more beneficial to clutch at holding on to positive feelings than negative ones. Nonattachment to positive and negative feelings is an essential part of growth. It allows you to see that you are more than your feelings. It also provides an opportunity to open your heart and mind to expressing your true essence, your soul's light, in physical life. That is your purpose here.

We are pleased you are more grounded, directed, and upbeat after today's work. We'll say goodbye for now, but that is only an expression. Even when your focus shifts to other things, we are still with you at all times. There are no restrictions of time or space in spirit. Our help, our guidance, our support are always available for the asking.

Personal Reflections

Today's lesson was a welcome reminder of a powerful coping tool for detaching from negative feelings that I have taught others and benefited from myself.

As on most days over the past three months with my inner teacher, I was definitely more centered after today's session. Simply sitting with my most uncomfortable feeling, observing it without judgment, without trying to change it, allowed me to detach from the feeling. It lost its hold as I accepted its presence. I was able to experience it as a passing feeling separate from myself.

There's a lot to be said for having your own internal therapist—a wise, inner source of knowledge that is clear, objective, helpful, accepting, nonjudgmental . . . and always available. My inner teacher provides a superb role model in this respect. Her very presence conveys a deep care and calm that inspires me. Yet, she is detached from judgment or any particular outcome. There is no pressure, no imposition of her views or expectations in the conditional, critical way often seen in human relationships. As I listen to her thoughts perceived internally, I sense the pure clarity of her thinking and feel permeated by her loving acceptance. Words cannot describe the expansiveness of this experience that is enlivened with an all-encompassing sense of peace and unconditional love.

My own attachment to feelings remains commonplace enough that I will benefit from continuing use of this simple tool for detaching from strong negative and positive emotions. I notice the tendency to want to hold on to positive feelings because they feel good and to push away those that are negative and uncomfortable. Either of these responses, however, gives power and control to my feelings which do not define my true Self and are, in fact, only temporary experiences. Learning to observe and detach from emotional responses, without judging them, facilitates growth. It presents opportunities to master feelings and become more aware of our eternal Self, the soul, as separate from its temporary body.

This process of observing our mind's thoughts and feelings as passing scenery and returning to our intended inner focus is familiar to those who meditate regularly. The benefits of this focused concentration—nonattachment to passing thoughts and feelings and discovery of the large mind of spirit as separate from the small mind of ego—are enormous and life changing.

LESSON
FORTY-FOUR

The Value of Cultivating Meaningful Friendships

1/10/2007, 9:00 a.m., Lesson Forty-Four

The absence of your weekly get together with a close friend has made you aware of the importance of consistent companionship and sharing with those you trust. Making time to cultivate these relationships is essential. *[My teacher acknowledges my humorous association of her word cultivate with the mechanical farm cultivator I was accustomed to from growing up on a farm.]* Just as a plow turns over the soil in preparation for planting and nurturing the growth of seedlings, so too the soil underlying meaningful friendships requires loving care, time, and attention if these relationships are to flourish.

Keeping the soil rich, loose, properly watered, planted with a good seed stock, and free of weeds helps nurture growing, healthy crops as well as relationships. The nurturing of friendship requires acceptance of and respect for each person's uniqueness; listening without judging; speaking your truth directly and honestly in ways that do not cause harm; honoring others' choices without attempting to control or manipulate them; valuing and loving the other for who and what they are rather than what they can do for you; sharing humor and emotional support; insuring a safe atmosphere for personal disclosure and sharing; and committing regular time and attention to the relationship.

You are inclined to be too self-reliant and to put work and other obligations before time with friends. Examine this and how it's working or not. Since relying on yourself is not an issue for you, it may be wise to develop your connection with friends and open yourself to receiving as well as giving in your relationships. *[I agree that balance is important.]*

You're beginning to be more open to this as evidenced by initiating more conversations and contact with others. You've enjoyed time with three new couples during your travels with your husband as a result of this. Do more of this with both individuals and couples and notice what happens. *[My doing more of this has resulted in several new, close friendships that offer mutual support, enjoyable activities, and stimulating conversation. I'm grateful to have a group of friends committed to personal and spiritual growth.]*

Do not isolate yourself from others outside the family and do not look only to family to meet your needs. Birth family relationships are only one source of companionship, support, closeness, and love. Your family is much broader than your birth family, marriage partner, and family by marriage. Friends outside of family and marriage offer something unique. Too much time with work and other obligations and too little self-care, including time with good friends, is a recipe for burnout and feeling cut off from the human family at large. Time with special friends is restorative. *[I can vouch for that.]*

Personal Reflections

I have been fortunate to have friendships in which there is mutual give and take, honesty, and trust that allow a deep level of sharing and enjoyment of our unique personalities and gifts. The support, love, and humor present in these friendships definitely relieve stress for me and are a vast source of learning about love, forgiveness, laughter, and kindness.

Each Is Part of and Contributes to the Whole

1/22/2007, 11:00 a.m., Lesson Forty-Five

After all this time, you are still concerned that the information and knowledge shared in this way is limited and will eventually dry up. That reflects your attitude of limitation. There is <u>so</u> much more than any of you know or can see from the physical world. Once you begin to get a glimmer of this, you will better understand our humor at your concern that the well of information from this end will dry up. The vastness of life, its laws, and plans unfolding throughout the universe are beyond comprehension while you are in physical form. Yet it is so.

As long as you open your heart and mind to the continuous unfolding of the magnificence of the Creator of All, there will be an unending supply of knowledge, experience, and growth. It is not possible to know or understand everything. That is a process of continuous evolution in both the physical and spirit dimensions. The Creator of All is not limited. All things are possible. Perceived limitations arise from our imperfect knowledge and lack of oneness with the Universal Source.

You still tend to measure and evaluate things in an egocentric way, looking at how they will affect you, your life, your goals, your desires. This is a false view of life's meaning. It is as limited in its perspective as your underlying fear that knowledge in the form of these lessons is limited.

You are part of the whole. The meaning of your being and life are best seen in that perspective. Your thoughts, behavior, and actions affect the whole, including all other living things, just as all living things affect you.

Everything, including thoughts, is energy and vibration. Your individual evolution and growth are affected by the whole and also contribute to the evolution of all living things in their collective journey to return to their Source. The infinite vastness of this continuous process, the universal laws that govern it, and the guided direction of all aspects of this evolution are awesome but difficult to comprehend while in physical form. Still, it is so.

The separateness perceived by you in physical life is not present in the life of spirit. You as an individual cannot grow and evolve in physical life without others growing just as others cannot evolve without your growth. All individuals contribute to the whole. The growth of all parts is needed to complete the whole in the journey of evolution back to the One.

Personal Reflections

These are inspiring and elusive concepts for me to grasp. Yet, I intuitively sense this truth of the oneness of all life, each of us part of and affecting the whole as well as being affected by each part and the whole. Living life from this perspective gives new meaning to the term the human family. It seems that our evolution as individuals is also interconnected. The growth of one of us affects everyone, and the growth of everyone is needed to complete the whole.

Though it is not the purpose of this book to discuss the ever evolving scientific theories and research that provide a base of knowledge to help understand metaphysical concepts such as nonlocal consciousness as well as the oneness and interconnection of all life, there are many writers who do so. A few of these resources, appropriate for lay audiences, are listed in the appendix. Using the concepts, theories, and research of modern science, these writers present ways to understand abstract concepts such as the web of life or web of interconnections; energy field; morphic resonance; zero point energy; holographic universe; nonlocal consciousness; remote healing; the akashic records; quantum or akashic consciousness.

The interconnection of all life, the illusion of separateness, and the vastness of the evolutionary plan of which we are a part are much easier for me to grasp and experience during intuitive journaling because it is all directly intuited with the nonphysical senses. The task, then, is to carry over that awareness and experiential perspective of these otherwise abstract concepts into physical life. These intuited experiences of oneness and interconnection with all of life in every form and dimension, whether visible or invisible, increase my awareness of times I'm acting separate from others, nature, and the world so I can shift my perspective back to one in which I am part of an interconnected whole. This offers a vast array of opportunities to learn and practice a more wholistic way of being in the world: sharing resources; seeking peaceful, equitable solutions when conflict arises; acting with kindness, gratitude, respect, and positive regard for myself, others, and nature; reconciling differences with fairness; and forgiving self and others for imperfections and mistakes. It is a life-enriching experience when I am able to do so in even the smallest way.

LESSON FORTY-SIX

Living from the Light Within

1/23/2007, 10:15 a.m., Lesson Forty-Six

The sunshine draws your attention, as it is meant to. The light of the sun is calming, restorative, and energizing. That is part of the reason you like being outside. The sun, and the many ways it sustains humans and life on earth, is most often taken for granted. It is such a constant in your lives and so dependable that it is in the background of your awareness. Yet, without it there would be no way to create and sustain growth on earth. The light of the sun is truly life giving. Its constancy and perpetual presence are examples of qualities of spirit that humans need to develop, practice, and manifest in their physical lives. Manifesting light and love as brightly, surely, and selflessly as the sun serves all life on earth. *[I found this to be a powerful statement of our purpose in human life—to manifest our*

205

soul's light and love in service to all life as selflessly as the sun shares its light with us.]

The life-giving sun does not hide or withhold its light out of fear, anger, resentment, or disappointment at being taken for granted, forgotten, or ignored by humans. So too, do not hide your light or allow it to dim in reaction to passing negative thoughts and feelings or lack of expected appreciation and recognition from others.

Your energy is purest when you are following your own path, the light within that manifests as intuition. Letting your light shine means being true to who and what you are, making choices based on that, not on what pleases others or what is most comfortable. It's not necessary to feel threatened by others' resistance to your views. Quiet persistence and assertion of your feelings and needs in a context of respect for others are all that's needed. *[As my teacher says this, I can simultaneously sense the powerful, quiet strength inherent in such an assured alignment with the soul within and the humility reflected in respect for others.]*

Following the light within is not contingent on others' approval. To make it so is to operate from fear. This dims your light and contributes to your loss of awareness of and connection with your Divine Light within. It is up to each of you to follow your own light within, your connection with the Source of All, or to stay lost and mired in the desires, wants, and feelings of the physical self as if that is what is real or true.

Remember, what is real and true is that you are spiritual beings in physical form for the purpose of manifesting your spirit's light and love in daily life. This is a gradual learning process and cannot be rushed, bought, sidestepped, or done for you by anyone else. It is not dependent on the approval of others. Connecting with and manifesting the light and love of your spirit is fostered through the patient perseverance of living from an open heart and mind.

Personal Reflections

Having desires, wants, and feelings are a natural part of being human. They are neither inherently good nor bad. They simply reflect aspects of creative power we each possess. It seems to me the choice that faces each of us is whether we will express desires and feelings in ways that align with the higher Self or with the physical ego self.

When I am expressing desires and feelings from my physical ego self, I am coming from small mind, a place that identifies itself with exclusion and separation and is bent on satisfying desires of me-mine or having my own way, sometimes without regard for others. When I am able to express desires and feelings in ways that reflect the inclusive mind of alignment with my higher Self, I am genuinely kind, compassionate, and helpful. In essence, I treat my fellow travelers on the path as I would wish to be treated in the same circumstances. Expressions of unconditional love in our physical lives are always from the higher Self. Though compassionate, forgiving, and nonjudgmental, unconditional love is not wishy-washy or submissive. Its clarity and strength are reflected in the ability to take firm stands, set clear boundaries, and convey constructive criticism while remaining respectful and kind.

I do not find it particularly helpful to think of the cravings, wishes, and feelings of the physical ego self as the enemy. Rather, I prefer to view them as reminders to look within at what needs to be faced and changed for my growth as a spiritual being. Examining beneath our material mask, in this way, allows us to open to the heart-mind of the soul that is seeking to express its divine qualities within physical matter. In awakening to the awareness that our true Self does not equate with the small mind desires and feelings of the physical ego self, we can allow our choices and responses to the ego self to be guided by our intentional alignment with the soul's light within. This acknowledges that the physical body-mind is a vehicle for the soul to express its inherent qualities of unconditional love and peace in physical form—to spiritualize matter—in its evolutionary journey to oneness with universal consciousness or Source.

Barbara Marx Hubbard calls this process—of shifting our primary identification from our separated physical ego self to our higher Self—emergence (also the title of her book).

For me, a consistent meditation practice has been invaluable in revealing this ego-focused small mind and building awareness that the choice of how I respond to its wants and feelings is within my control. The witness mind developed through meditation over time could not help but observe the seemingly relentless wishes and feelings of the ego self. Eventually, the awareness emerged that the observing mind of my higher Self was not the same as the ego's insistent wants. The value of self-discipline took on new meaning as I better understood its central role in evolving toward living from the higher Self with its inclusive perspective and its higher order ideals rather than the ego self's desires.

Today's lesson suggests that whether we live from the soul's light within or remain stuck in our mistaken identification with our physical ego self is indeed a choice faced by each of us on our learning path. I liked the reminder that this is a gradual learning process that cannot be rushed, bypassed, or turned over to someone else. Patient perseverance in living from an open heart-mind strengthens our connection with and expression of our soul's peace and love. For me, this is fostered by awareness of my true identity as spirit in physical form; gratitude; forgiveness; care for all life; self-responsibility; developing and sharing my gifts and talents; spiritual practices such as meditation; stepping outside the perspective of the separate, individual self to see the bigger picture of we as one whole; acknowledging there is always a bigger picture and purpose that I cannot see; reminding myself that what I do to others is also done to self, and similarly, what I do to self is done to others.

LESSON FORTY-SEVEN

Creating Peace

1/24/2007, 8:50 a.m., Lesson Forty-Seven

Today's subject is peace. There is ample evidence in the lives of each of you throughout the world of the effects of peaceful and nonpeaceful behavior.

Peace, or the lack of it, is created, fostered, and manifested from within each of you. The making of peace begins within your thoughts, attitudes, feelings, and responses to life. Peace is cultivated from an open, compassionate, loving heart that sees the oneness of all living things. A peaceful attitude is one in which life events are viewed and interpreted in a cooperative, collaborative way, and the needs of all are honestly and equally honored. Peaceful behavior requires the willingness to share resources as well as the courage to persevere in resolving conflict in ways that serve all. This begins first within each of you in your attitude and behavior toward self and others.

Hatred, aggression, violence, fear, greed, jealousy, and dishonesty all close the heart and generate behavior and actions that do harm to self, others, and the world. The reality that these feelings and attitudes begin within and manifest outward gives you each tremendous power to change your inner world to reflect peace and love in the outer world. The power you each have in every moment to choose peace and love or hatred and fear is a responsibility and an opportunity to do your part in bringing about a peaceful world. This, too, is a process. Have faith and strength to persevere in doing your part regardless of others' choices. All are on the same path. Though you differ in where you are on the path, the part of each in the whole is of equal importance.

Today, practice a peaceful attitude toward yourself and others by being gentle, kind, and nonjudgmental. Smile and radiate warm, positive feelings from your heart. To the best of your ability, be peace. And for all the moments of today, recognize other's peaceful behavior. When negative feelings arise, use this process to transform their energy: mentally observe and acknowledge the negative feelings without judgment; choose to release the negative feelings; open your heart and allow the heart's love and compassion to be stronger than your negative feelings; mentally reframe the problem as an opportunity to practice a peaceful response; and identify a constructive response. Listen from the heart's love and compassion for ideas on how best to dissolve the stressful situation.

Personal Reflections

Have you noticed how challenging it is to sustain this peaceful way of relating to life? How easy it is to revert to faultfinding, unkind, or annoyed reactions when you don't like something or someone? This lesson made me realize how little I understood the far-reaching effects of my inner thoughts and attitudes. I have not often considered the perspective my inner teacher is presenting: that I, and each of us, have tremendous power and opportunity to create peace or nonpeace in the outside world through our moment-to-moment choices within; that peace or its opposite begins within each of us and reflects outward.

Creating peace requires an open heart and an ability to observe our inner and outer responses in a detached, nonjudgmental way. Recognizing and accepting responsibility for our own nonpeaceful ways are necessary if we are to transform their negative energy. It is a way of being in the world that I admire when I notice it in someone else's kindness, good humor, patience, nonattachment to being right, and ability to listen to and genuinely value other's ideas that are different from their own.

Today's lesson included a process for transforming the energy of negative emotions that is reminiscent of the Institute of HeartMath's wonderful tools for changing stressful, negative emotions. I have used them personally and taught them to patients with excellent results. They are easy to learn, very effective, and congruent with the life view related in these intuitive lessons. I have listed two books co-authored by Doc Childre in the bibliography that describe the HeartMath tools and how to apply them.

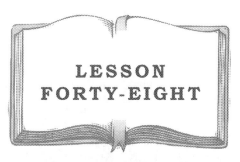

LESSON FORTY-EIGHT

Moving On

1/25/2007, 9:25 a.m., Lesson Forty-Eight

It is now time to end these lessons and move on to the process of transcribing, editing, and seeing this work through to publication. The work will then be available to those who are ready to use it to further their own growth. They will use and practice the ideas as they choose.

Take each piece of the remaining work needed to bring this to completion and have fun with it. Use and trust your judgment throughout this process.

Notice how you have let go of needing to know who and what I am. It is no longer important, is it? You are certain that the source is true, loving, compassionate, and nonjudgmental. Others will decide for themselves whether it rings true for them and is of value in their own growth.

You have done your part. We are grateful for your opening your heart and mind to our efforts to further your and others' spiritual growth and development.

Personal Reflections

The lessons over the past two weeks contained preparatory messages regarding the nearing completion of this endeavor. Still, I was not prepared for today's formal ending of these intuitive lessons. Now it is time to begin the next phase of making this available to others. I appreciated the help given in breaking down the work of publication into manageable steps.

The patient encouragement given by my inner teacher in the years that followed these lessons helped me move through recurring fears and doubts to complete this book. By then, I understood that these lessons given from spirit were not only for my benefit but also for others working on their spiritual growth. Despite this, my inner teacher clearly conveyed that the choice about whether or not to publish these lessons was entirely mine. There was no hint of pressure or expectation. I was free to choose as I saw fit. There are no words that come close to describing this level of genuine acceptance, trust, and nonattachment.

My inner teacher assured me this connection with the world of spirit for the purpose of aiding my growth and learning would always be available. I continue to use intuitive journaling and benefit from its lessons. It evolves as I put into practice what I'm learning.

Rereading the lessons is always valuable. I am either reminded of ways to live from the higher Self that I may have lost sight of as I slipped back into old habits or I grasp a deeper layer of meaning that I can begin applying. In this way, the learning and growth are ongoing. When the current level of awareness is integrated, the next layer of learning appears and the work of practice and assimilation begins again in a repeating cycle. This is by no means an easy, smooth, or consistently forward progression. The important thing seems to be to keep on applying what I know in the best way possible.

As I look back at how I've put into practice what I've learned so far, I realize the changes I consider most important are my increased awareness of when I am creating fear and negativity and the positive shifts in my thinking and attitudes. In particular, I am more focused on living from an open heart, being grateful and appreciative throughout the day.

To maintain balance and regulate stress constructively, I use intuitive journaling as well as the following practices I've mentioned before: the various deep breathing exercises described within the lessons; tapping, the energy treatment approach using Emotional Freedom Techniques, in combination with positive affirmations; meditation; yoga exercises with a conscious integration of breath with slow movement and gratitude for the body; reframing negative thoughts and feelings; healthy eating habits; Reiki healing touch; outdoor activities; and time with family and friends.

I notice I am less fearful in general and more consciously aware of doubts and fears when they resurface. As I am much less likely to identify with negative or fearful thoughts, I can more easily detect their underlying erroneous conclusions and reframe them to a more balanced, empowered perspective. As a result, I am more aware of the power of my thought choices and am therefore less controlled by negative thoughts and feelings.

One of the most significant changes is my acceptance of my inner teacher and her wise, compassionate guidance without having to know the exact details of who and what she is. I see more clearly now that my initial curiosity about these details was an ego-based distraction from directly experiencing and acknowledging this inner connection and communication between my higher Self and the world of spirit.

What is important is the certainty of knowing that accompanied this direct experience. The expansive, infinite qualities of my higher Self and the spiritual dimension unfettered by time or space, together with the pervasive qualities of peace, all encompassing love, compassion, and wisdom were profound.

It took a long time for me to understand that because we are all part of the oneness of universal consciousness, my higher Self was able to connect and communicate with my inner teacher from spirit. Once I was able to wrap my mind around the truth that all of life is part of this infinite oneness, it was more evident that we are all connected to the whole, no matter what plane of consciousness we inhabit.

Grasping the interactive and mutual growth-enhancing qualities of this working partnership with my inner teacher took even longer for me to fully grasp. It was only in rereading the lessons that I began to fully comprehend that the help given by this group of souls in spirit to foster my growth and the spiritual lessons they are offering others through me are part of their soul contract for fulfilling their purpose and evolving their growth in spirit (lessons twenty-seven and thirty-six).

Overall, this direct experience of the spiritual dimension and communication with my inner teacher in spirit heightened my awareness of the importance of alignment with and living from my higher Self, the soul's light of love, to the best of my ability in physical life. It also brought home in a much deeper, meaningful way that I am more than my physical body. My true Self is infinite, eternal spirit.

Knowing that I can choose to remain connected to and communicate with this interpenetrating dimension of spirit, my home, through my higher Self while in physical life is an awakening of its own. Knowing that wise help and guidance are always available and that we all serve unique purposes in the greater plan is as humbling as it is enlivening and inspiring.

Epilogue

Lessons is based on intuitive communication with my teachers in spirit. This was activated through use of intention to connect with my higher Self and the choice to open my heart-mind to the highest wisdom for the purpose of spiritual growth. Intuitive journaling was the tool for recording the knowledge received. My higher Self led me exactly where I needed to go: to connect and communicate with wise teachers in spirit for our mutual evolving growth.

These lessons are universal and timeless. They are not new or unique to me. Though universally relevant, they simultaneously speak to the current life circumstances and needs of the writer. Inner guidance uses who and where we are now in our personal and spiritual development to encourage our growth. It never goes beyond what we can handle or use; just enough to stretch us out of our comfort zone so we keep learning and evolving.

Intuitive journaling is a conscious, deliberate way of accessing our own inner wisdom and guidance for the purpose of growing spiritually. Spiritual growth and personal psychological growth go hand in hand. This is true regardless of the form your spiritual practice takes. So, when you begin intuitive journaling, expect any unaddressed or unresolved personal issues to arise. Difficult as it may be, this is a gift. It provides an opportunity to know ourselves more deeply, to take charge of our growth, and to learn to live from our soul's unique light of love, our higher Self.

Although this book is completed, its lessons are ongoing. Even now, rereading these lessons from seven years ago is beneficial. I still use intuitive journaling nearly every day. It provides insights and wise guidance for whatever is most needed right then in ways I can never anticipate or predict. I learn something new every time from a much larger, expanded perspective. The knowledge is given in a way I can understand and use to aid my growth. Most important, the experience of infinite compassion, peace, care, kindness, patience, humor, and lightness that accompanies this wise guidance is indescribably inspiring.

I continue to use intuitive journaling to help interpret dreams and intuitive images arising spontaneously or during Reiki healing touch. It's also very useful if I am stuck in some negative way of responding to everyday situations or relationships. It provides a more constructive, big picture view of stressful situations and relationships, pointing out my part in the problem and what I can do to change it for the better. It never belittles anyone, no matter how angry I might be at someone. I can see how the guidance given heightens awareness of and connection with my higher Self and universal consciousness. It gives a wider angle view of what needs to be learned from trying situations.

Intuitive journaling can also be used to help with small and large decisions. It's like checking in with a wise, neutral inner advisor who has access to a vast data base guided by a Divine cosmic plan that considers potential options from the perspective of the highest good of all. I have found intuitive journaling helpful in guiding my choices regarding health-related concerns, this book, and new interests and activities. Since I am responsible for all my decisions, I do my homework before I check in with inner guidance. I collect any information needed, examine all the options, and weigh the pros and cons of each alternative.

My inner teacher(s) from spirit saw intuitive journaling and *Lessons* as a working partnership. My part was to show up consistently with a sincere, clear intention to connect and communicate with the highest wisdom through my higher Self; open my heart-mind to receiving the information; make an accurate written record; use the knowledge to grow personally and spiritually; and make these lessons available to others. Their part was to use this daily format to communicate the highest wisdom that would foster my spiritual growth and fulfillment of my purposes. In doing so, they fulfilled part of their soul contract for their own ongoing growth and learning in spirit. Through this book, my inner teacher(s) also fulfilled another part of their purpose—to communicate these lessons from spirit to others in physical life.

Since I am an advocate of teaching others how to access their own intuitive guidance for themselves, it was also important to convey the steps I used for intuitive journaling. You can try it out, if you choose, and modify it to suit you. Whatever format you decide to use, keep in mind that intention, protection, and an open heart-mind matter. From my perspective, they affect the level and clarity of information received.

If, like me, you have difficulty believing such wisdom could come from within you through your higher Self, notice your disbelief and doubts then release them whenever they arise. By applying and using your own constructive, wise ideas that come from within through intuitive journaling, you will see for yourself whether the results are beneficial or not.

Try to let go of expectations about the form your inner guidance will take and simply stay open to noticing what happens. Because we are each unique, our intuitive guidance expresses itself uniquely too. One way is not better than another.

Avoid the ego trap of getting enamored with the way in which your higher Self's wisdom is communicated. You saw an example of this in my initially getting caught up in the distraction of who/what my inner teacher was. The inner wisdom and lessons that are conveyed for your unique soul growth and your trying to integrate these lessons into your daily life is what matters. Other variations of this ego trap include getting puffed up by what you learn; acting from an inflated sense of self-importance; trying to impose what you learn on others; and seeing your way as right and others as wrong.

Learning to discern whether the source of your intuitive guidance is from the ego self or your higher Self takes honest self-reflection, knowledge of yourself, humility, and the sincere intention to set aside the limited ego mind to connect only with the highest wisdom through your higher Self. Since we are imperfect, our egos can and do intrude.

Expect this. Observe the ways your ego distracts from and interferes with connecting with your higher Self.

Signs that you have connected with an aspect of the ego self rather than the higher Self include receiving a critical, belittling, demanding, destructive, judgmental, or angry voice. Exclusive messages that flatter you or set you apart as special or better than others also reflect the ego self.

You can recognize your own higher Self or inner teacher(s) from spirit by their qualities of kindness, compassion, nonjudgment, humility, acceptance, and unconditional love. These qualities will extend to all beings and all life in an open, inclusive way with no exceptions. Respect for you, others, and all life will be evident at all times.

The information and guidance received through your higher Self will have a distinct clarity that will often seem simple yet profound at the same time.

Your higher Self will never encourage any form of harm to self or others. It will not judge, criticize, use anger or guilt or threats to control you or your choices.

Though your higher Self may offer ideas, if asked, it will not tell you what to do; it leaves all choices and decisions to you.

Your higher Self will always foster self-responsibility. Though the choices and work are ours, the higher Self encourages, supports, and empowers our healthy growth in all areas.

When the higher Self offers input in response to your asking, it will not force information on you, demand, or mandate how things will be. It will not get caught up in your emotional drama or take sides. In fact, the higher

Self provides guidance congruent with the highest good for all and acknowledges a greater Divine power and help available from spirit in response to our requests. It operates within a larger, guided framework of the Divine plan.

When you begin putting into practice some of the things you learn through intuitive journaling, you'll also be able to assess whether or not the results of your effort are helpful to your growth. Changes that foster your alignment with and living from your higher Self may not be easy and will likely evolve gradually, but you will know when the changes are healthy and beneficial.

Whether you use intuitive journaling or some other way to connect with and learn to live from your higher Self, it is a consciously chosen process of change, one in which we are active participants in our evolving growth at all levels—physical, mental-emotional, and spiritual.

My hope is that you enjoy your journey in learning to consciously tune in to your own inner wisdom. It is an inspiring, hope-filled journey. Enjoy each step along the way. Be patient with yourself and the process, especially when you lose your forward momentum and regress to outworn, negative habits. Dedicate yourself to doing your part as faithfully as you can. Remember to not overdo it—moderation and balance are important. More is not better; overdoing can overwhelm our ability to integrate and assimilate new learning. Know that your own unique lessons will unfold at the right time and in the ways that are best for you.

Namaste
The spirit within me honors the spirit within you.
When you are in that place within you
and I am in that place within me,
we are one.

Appendix

Resources Relating Concepts of
Science and Metaphysics

This addendum to chapter forty-five lists some of my favorite references for understanding scientific theories and research as they relate to abstract, metaphysical concepts such as the oneness and interconnection of all life, universal memory, consciousness surviving death, angels, distance healing, and paranormal phenomena. These include books by P.M.H. Atwater (*The Big Book of Near-Death Experiences* and *Near-Death Experiences, The Rest of the Story*); Gregg Braden *(The Spontaneous Healing of Belief* and *The Divine Matrix*)*; Matthew Fox and Rupert Sheldrake (*The Physics of Angels*); Ervin Laszlo (*Science and the Akashic Field: An Integral Theory of Everything* and *The Akashic Experience*); Lynn McTaggart (*The Field, The Quest for the Secret Force of the Universe* and *The Intention Experiment*); Belleruth Naparstek (*Your Sixth Sense*); Judith Pennington *(Your Psychic Soul*); Gary Schwartz and Linda Russek (*The Living Energy Universe*); Russell Targ (*Do You See What I See*); and Kevin Todeschi (*Edgar Cayce on the Akashic Records*).

In *The Physics of Angels,* Rupert Sheldrake points out that the quantum-matter, electromagnetic, and gravitational fields currently recognized by orthodox science all interpenetrate and do not interfere with one another. He goes on to comment that "the idea of angels as fieldlike allows us to see how they too can interpenetrate." (p. 42) To me, this implies that the invisible world of spirit interpenetrates the visible physical world, making two-way extrasensory communication possible in a variety of ways, including intuitive journaling.

Russell Targ describes a number of examples in *Do You See What I See* whose common theme is "that awareness persists, and that our minds are *powerful* and *nonlocal*. And above all, we are more than just a body. Our memories and our present thoughts affect the thoughts and experiences of ourselves and others now and in the future. Our memories, emotions, and intentions create information that can be accessed in non-ordinary states of awareness, such as dreams and remote viewing." (p. 233)

Direct, intuitive experience of this nonlocal, infinite mind unlimited by time or space during intuitive journaling is incredibly freeing, expansive, and immediate. Words cannot do it justice.

P.M.H. Atwater, in her book *Near-Death Experiences*, comments "physicists are moving closer to the idea that, at the quantum level, all minds are part of each other, entangled in a giant web of interconnections streaming from a common source. The idea that anything can be separate, that distance can ensure separation, is untrue. Once paths cross, even slightly, what affects the one will affect the other." (p. 149)

In his 7/27/2012 blog titled "Akashic Think . . . World Changing" posted on the worldshiftinternational.org website in the Science and Spirituality section, Ervin Laszlo refers to akashic consciousness as "a consciousness that I am part of this wholeness. I am part of the world, and the world is part of me." He comments that this is not wishful thinking but has a scientific basis. Laszlo notes a rising new paradigm in the sciences based on "a paradigm of inclusive, intrinsic, and immediate oneness." In the same blog, Laszlo refers to this as the Akasha Paradigm which "tells us we live in an interconnected, intrinsically non-local world . . . . Every single thing makes a lasting impression on the whole world."

The akashic record is said to contain every word, thought, event, deed, and intent of every living being. Kevin Todeschi in *Edgar Cayce on the Akashic Records* states these records are interactive in nature and influence our daily lives, relationships, feelings, beliefs, and the potentials we draw to ourselves (p. xii). I think of these records as a dynamic, interactive, invisible cosmic data bank. In his above-mentioned book, Todeschi cites case files of Edgar Cayce, known as the sleeping prophet, accessing the akashic records to help others.

Laszlo, in *The Akashic Experience*, theorizes that people access this akashic field through a process of quantum resonance between the brain and the quantum hologram of the field (p. 251). He theorizes that distance or remote healing by energy healers, the effectiveness of which has been established in studies, results from the healer's brain entering a relation of quantum resonance with the healee's brain and body (p. 252). As author Judith Pennington phrased it so eloquently in *Your Psychic Soul*, "Clear spiritual intention enables the soul to resonate with the non-local energy and information in the quantum sea of light that permeates and interpenetrates all of reality."(p. 45)

In *Your Sixth Sense*, Belleruth Naparstek notes the association between regular meditation and increasing intuitive awareness or psychic abilities (p. 106). She explains the physics of extrasensory perception, love, and imagery using concepts of modern physics, particularly the theories of David Bohm and Itzhak Bentov. She writes, "We have the ability to dissolve our fixed boundaries and expand into and merge with those things that we normally see as *other* by deliberately generating feelings of love, gratitude, and universal oneness." (p. 96)

Bibliography

Atwater, P.M.H. *Near-Death Experiences: The Rest of the Story.* Charlottesville: Hampton Roads Publishing Company, 2011.

—. *The Big Book of Near-Death Experiences.* Charlottesville: Hampton Roads Publishing Company, 2007.

Borysenko, Joan. "Appendix of Meditation Practices." In *Pocketful of Miracles,* by Joan Borysenko, 11; 413-424. New York: Warner Books, Inc, 1994.

Braden, Gregg. *The Divine Matrix.* Carlsbad: Hay House, Inc, 2009.

—. *The Spontaneous Healing of Belief.* Carlsbad: Hay House, Inc, 2008.

Brennan, Barbara Ann. *Hands of Light.* New York: Bantam Books, 1988.

Bryan, Mark with Cameron, Julia, and Allen, Catherine. *The Artist's Way At Work.* New York: Quill, 1999.

Callahan, Roger. *Callahan Techniques Thought Field Therapy.* www.rogercallahan.com.

Cameron, Julia. *The Artist's Way.* New York: Tarcher, 1992.

Childre, Doc, and Martin, Howard. *The HeartMath Solution.* San Francisco: HarperSanFrancisco, 2000.

Childre, Doc, and Rozman, Deborah. *Transforming Anger.* Oakland: New Harbinger Publications, Inc, 2003.

Craig, Gary. *Official EFT website of Gary Craig.* www. emofree.com.

DiMaggio, Joanne. "Inspirational Writing: Tool for Transformation." *Venture Inward,* April-June 2011: 16-19.

Fox, Matthew, and Sheldrake, Rupert. *The Physics of Angels.* San Francisco: HarperSanFrancisco, 1996.

Gawain, Shakti. "Earth is our collective body." In *Reflections in the Light,* by Shakti Gawain, December 9 entry. San Rafael: New World Library, 1990.

—. *The Living in the Light Workbook.* Novato: Nataraj Publishing, 1998.

Hanh, Thich Nhat. "Conscious Breathing." In *Peace Is Every Step,* by Thich Nhat Hanh, 8-11. New York: Bantam Books, 1992.

Hubbard, Barbara Marx. *Emergence.* San Francisco: Hampton Roads Publishing Co, 2012.

Laszlo, Ervin. "Akashic Think . . . World Changing." *worldshiftinternational.org* blog in *Science and Spirituality.* July 27, 2012.

—. *Science and the Akashic Field.* Rochester: Inner Traditions, 2007.

—. *The Akashic Experience.* Rochester: Inner Traditions, 2009.

McTaggart, Lynne. *The Field.* New York: HarperCollins, 2008.

—. *The Intention Experiment.* New York: Free Press, 2008.

Myss, Caroline. *Caroline Myss.* www.myss.com.

Nani, Christel. *Diary of a Medical Intuitive.* Cayucos: L.M.Press, 2005.

—. *Guidance 24/7.* Phoenix: Queens Court Press, 2009.

Nani, Christel. *Transforming Your Archetypes (CD).* 2006.

Naparstek, Belleruth. *Your Sixth Sense.* New York: Harper Collins, 1997.

Orloff, Judith. *Judith Orloff M.D.* www.drjudithorloff.com.

Pennington, Judith. www.JudithPennington.com.

—. *Your Psychic Soul.* Virginia Beach: 4th Dimension Press, 2012.

Puryear, Herbert B. "Meditation." In *The Edgar Cayce Primer*, by Herbert B. Puryear, 146. New York: Bantam Books, 1982.

Reed, Henry. *Channeling Your Higher Self.* Virginia Beach: A.R.E. Press, 2008.

Rossman, Martin L. *Guided Imagery for Self-Healing.* Tiburon: H J Kramer Inc, 2000.

Schulz, Mona Lisa. *Awakening Intuition.* New York: Harmony Books, 1998.

Schwartz, Gary E.R., and Russek, Linda G.S. *The Living Energy Universe.* Charlottesville: Hampton Roads Publishing Co, 1999.

Shealy, Norman. *Dr. Norm Shealy Self-Health Systems.* www.normshealy.com.

Targ, Russell. *Do You See What I See.* Hampton Roads Publishing Company, Inc, 2010.

Todeschi, Kevin J. *Edgar Cayce on the Akashic Records.* Virginia Beach: A.R.E. Press, 2010.

VanPraagh, James. *Heaven and Earth.* New York: Pocket Books, 2006.

—. *James Van Praagh.* www.vanpraagh.com.

Virtue, Doreen. *Divine Guidance.* Los Angeles: Renaissance Books, 1998.

—. *Divine Prescriptions.* Los Angeles: Renaissance Books, 2000.

Index

About the Author

Sharon Brunink received her doctorate in clinical psychology from Kent State University in 1976 and worked as a mental health provider in Colorado for thirty years. She has worked with adolescents, adults, and children in psychological treatment settings ranging from inpatient, residential and day treatment, and outpatient treatment in private practice. She retired from clinical practice in 2007 but continues to manage the administrative aspects of the psychology practice she shared with her colleague and husband, a rehabilitation psychologist. Since her professional retirement, she completed Reiki training, a form of healing touch, and enjoys practicing that on a volunteer basis. She also enjoys writing; traveling; a regular yoga and meditation practice; time with family and friends; cooking; bicycling, walking, and hiking; and learning new things. She lives in Colorado Springs with her husband, Tony Ricci.

She can be reached by e-mail at sabrunink@gmail.com

Printed in the United States
By Bookmasters